Roasting

Techniques for the perfect roast

Roasting
Techniques for the perfect roast

Rodney Dunn

whitecap

This edition published in Canada by Whitecap Books Ltd. For more information, contact

Whitecap Books
351 Lynn Avenue
North Vancouver, British Columbia, Canada
V7J 2C4

Created and produced by Lansdowne Publishing Pty Ltd,
CEO: Steven Morris, email: sales@lanspub.com.au

Commissioned by Deborah Nixon
Text: Rodney Dunn
Photographer: Alan Benson
Stylist: Jane Hann
Food preparation: Christine Chandler
Designer: Grant Slaney, Modern Art Production Group
Editor: Sharon Silva
Production Manager: Sally Stokes
Project Coordinator: Bettina Hodgson

All notations of errors or omissions should be addressed to Whitecap Books Ltd., Editorial Department, at the above address. All other correspondence (author inquiries, permissions, and rights) concerning the content of this book should be addressed to Lansdowne Publishing, Level 1, 18 Argyle Street, The Rocks NSW 2000, Australia.

ISBN 1-55285-586-4

Cataloging-in-Publication data available upon request

Set in Helvetica on Quark XPress
Printed in Singapore by Tien Wah Press (Pte) Ltd

1 2 3 4 5   08 07 06 05 04

Contents

Introduction

What is roasting?

The term "roasting" was originally used for what is now called "spit roasting." Meats were slowly turned over an open fire, with drip trays placed under them to catch any rendered fat. As the meats roasted, they were continually basted to prevent the exterior from drying out before the interior was cooked.

Today roasting is done in an uncovered, shallow pan in the dry heat of an oven. The modern oven, as opposed to an open fire, not only delivers gentler heat, but also allows cooks to maintain an even temperature and to regulate cooking time better. Roasting can be a time-consuming cooking method, but the preparation is often easy. Once the food is in the oven, it needs only minimal attention from the cook.

Choosing the best cut

When roasting meat, your first decision is the selection of an appropriate cut. Not every cut is suitable for roasting, of course, and it is wise to rely on your butcher to help you make a sound choice. In general, larger cuts cook more evenly in the steady, gentle heat of the oven than they do on the stove top.

Each cut comes from a different part of the animal, so each has been worked in slightly different ways. The cuts that have been worked the most, such as the shoulder (blade), chuck (neck), shanks (shins), and round (topside), will be tougher and should be slowly roasted. In other words, they are best cooked at a lower temperature for a longer time to break down the muscle fibers. A prime cut, such as tenderloin (fillet) or sirloin, benefits from cooking at a high temperature for a shorter amount of time, which browns the surface and leaves the interior juicy. Because they have a lower fat content, prime cuts dry out and toughen if cooked for extended periods.

A combination of heat levels can be used both for tender and tough cuts. You can start out the meat at a high temperature to give it a nicely browned exterior and then finish it at a moderate temperature. You can also do the reverse: cook it at a lower temperature to begin to reduce shrinkage and to keep it juicy, and then, not long before it is done, increase the heat to a high temperature to brown.

Finally, before selecting any cut, consider the number of people you are serving, whether you want a bone-in or boneless cut, and any time restrictions.

Using marinades and stuffings

It is always important to make food as flavorful as possible. When you are roasting, marinades and stuffings are the two most popular ways to impart flavor.

Marinades are liquid mixtures in which items to be roasted are soaked. They generally include an acid, such as wine or citrus juice, along with other flavorings. The acid, in addition to contributing flavor, works to break down connective tissue,

tenderizing the meat or poultry. It is important to remember that a marinade must have time to penetrate, therefore larger items typically need more marinating time. A variation on the marinade is the rub, a dry mixture of spices and other seasonings. The exterior of the food is lightly coated with oil, then the seasoning mixture is rubbed into the surface. The oil helps the rub adhere, and the seasonings impart flavor during the cooking.

While a marinade or rub is applied to the outside of foods, a stuffing is placed inside. It may be no more than lemon halves and rosemary sprigs slipped into the cavity of a chicken to add flavor and to help the bird keep its plump shape. Or, it can be a bread-, grain-, or meat-based stuffing with many ingredients and seasonings, which then becomes a side dish.

Trussing

Before roasting, some meats and poultry are secured into a compact shape, or trussed, for even cooking, as protruding pieces, such as poultry wings or the tips of drumsticks, can burn. Trussing can be as simple as tucking wing tips under and tying together poultry legs with kitchen string. If a bird is stuffed, trussing can sometimes involve a more complicated securing of the bird's shape (page 15). Tying a beef tenderloin (fillet) or pork loin will ensure the meat will keep its shape for neat carving, guaranteeing an attractive presentation.

Choosing the correct size pan

Using a properly sized pan will contribute to successful roasting. If the pan is too large, the juices will evaporate easily and scorch on the bottom. If it is too small and deep, the air will not circulate around the roast, causing the food to steam. This will result in a pale, insipid roast, and because steam is hotter than air, the roast will likely overcook. Select a shallow pan just large enough to accommodate the item to be roasted without crowding. Also,

always place the meat in the pan fat side up to protect the flesh from direct heat and so the melting fat will naturally baste the flesh.

Calibrating your oven

For foolproof roasting, the oven temperature must be accurate. Each oven is different, so getting to know your equipment is important. Purchase a good-quality oven thermometer and check to see that the dial setting and the heat match. If they don't, always remember to compensate for the discrepancy when you turn on the oven. Nearly every oven has hot spots; find them in yours and then rotate the roast as it cooks to compensate for them.

Browning and basting (glazing)

Many roasting recipes start with cooking the roast for a short period of time at a high temperature and then reducing the heat for the duration of the cooking. This browns the exterior of a meat roast and crisps the skin on poultry. Browning caramelizes the natural sugars, delivering an appealing textural contrast between the crisp outside and the juicy inside. This high-heat step can also be done by searing the meat in the roasting pan on the stove top before putting it in the oven to finish cooking.

You can build an even better crust on the meat by basting (glazing), which usually involves brushing or pouring the pan drippings over the meat at regular intervals during cooking. Sometimes, however, a specially made basting sauce is used. You can also brush or pour a separate sweet, sticky glaze over the roast before it goes into the oven and then regularly apply additional glaze during cooking, which results in a sweet, caramelized crust.

Testing for doneness

The hardest part of roasting is judging when the food is done. Roasting uses dry heat, which means that if the food is accidentally overcooked, it will be unpalatably dry. Therefore, knowing when roasted foods are done, yet still moist and succulent, is extremely important.

The simplest and easiest method for judging doneness is with a thermometer. There are two basic types. The so-called probe thermometer is sometimes inserted into the meat before it goes into the oven and remains there until the desired temperature is reached, or it can be thrust into the meat toward the end of cooking and left there until the temperature is reached. In contrast, the instant-read thermometer, which gives a reading within several seconds of being inserted, can only be used outside of the oven. No matter which type is used, it is important to insert it halfway into the food at its thickest point. The tip must not rest on either bone or fat, as both can skew the reading.

Once roasted meats and poultry are removed from the oven, they continue to cook from the residual heat, that is, the heat trapped in the roast. Therefore, they should register about 5 degrees Fahrenheit (2 or 3 degrees Celsius) below the desired temperature when tested for doneness; they will reach the desired temperature while they rest.

In the absence of a thermometer, make a small incision in the thickest part of a roast and check the color. Rare meat should be reddish, medium-rare meat should be pinkish, medium meat should be pale pink, and well-done meat should reveal no hint of pink. To check chicken and turkey for doneness, insert a thin, metal skewer or the tip of a knife into the thigh joint. The juices should run clear.

The more often you roast, the better you will become at judging doneness. In time, you will be able to tell when some roasts are done by their color or by the resistance you feel when you press them with a fingertip: the greater the resistance, the more well-done the meat is.

Deglazing

Deglazing a roasting pan captures the flavor and juices that have leached from the meat during cooking. To deglaze a pan, remove the excess fat, then place the pan over high heat on the stove top. Add liquid, such as wine or stock, bring to a brisk simmer, and scrape the pan bottom to loosen any browned bits. Continue to cook until the liquid is reduced, then strain it and serve it with the roast. For gravy, you will need to add flour to thicken the juices and then additional liquid. See page 17 for an illustrated guide to deglazing a pan and making gravy.

Resting, carving, and serving

Once the roast is cooked, it must rest before it can be carved. Cover it loosely with aluminum foil to keep it warm; a tight covering will cause it to steam. This resting period will allow the juices to redistribute throughout the meat, which will keep precious juices from escaping when the meat is cut.

Use a sharp knife to carve. A dull blade will require you to use too much pressure, which can force moisture out of the meat. In general, you should cut the meat across the grain into relatively thin slices. This will deliver a more tender slice, making the roast easier to eat.

A roast can be served in one of two ways. You can arrange it whole on a platter, perhaps with vegetables, or place it on the dining table and then carve and serve it in front of your guests. Or, you can carve the roast in the kitchen and arrange the slices on warmed dinner plates for serving.

Basic equipment for roasting

Roasting pans

Roasting pans come in a variety of sizes and are made from a variety of materials, from stainless steel to aluminum, glass, and porcelain. They should be solid enough not to buckle and durable enough to last.

Roasting racks

Roasting racks are placed inside a roasting pan to elevate the meat from the fat that collects on the base of the pan during cooking. They come in two varieties: a normal flat rack and an upright rack with sloping sides, called a "vertical rack," used for poultry.

Thermometers

Two types of thermometers can be used. Available in spring-action and liquid styles, the probe thermometer registers the slow rise of the interior temperature of a roast. (There is also the more costly digital probe, which includes a digital readout unit attached by a long, thin wire to the sensor inserted in the meat. The unit sits on the countertop next to the stove, making it possible to check the temperature with just a glance.) The instant-read thermometer, available in spring-action and digital models, is used near the end of cooking, outside of the oven. It registers the temperature within seconds of being inserted. See Testing for Doneness, pages 10–11, for additional information on how to use both thermometers.

Carving knives, forks, and steels

Carving knives need to be sharp and slightly flexible. Pointed knives are used to carve meat off the bone. Carving knives with rounded ends are called "slicers" and are used for boneless meat. Most knives now are made of stainless steel; in the past they were made from carbon steel, which is easy to sharpen and maintains a

sharp edge. However, these are harder to maintain, as the steel is prone to rust if not cared for properly.

Carving forks are used to hold the meat in place while carving. Forks generally have a guard to protect the hand while carving. Sharpening steels are sold with carving sets and are used to sharpen and hone the knife's edge.

Carving board
A thick wooden board is used to carve meat. It has a wooden groove around the edge to catch the meat juices.

Glazing brush
A glazing brush is essential for greasing pans and brushing meats and poultry with oil or marinades while cooking. Invest in a good-quality brush, as the poorer quality tend to lose bristles.

Cooking string
A good-quality unbleached cooking string is used to tie or truss meats, poultry, and fish before cooking. Wetting the string will prevent it from stretching during cooking.

Basic techniques (step by step)

Carving a leg of lamb

1 On a carving board, using a napkin or pair of tongs, hold the cooked leg of lamb at the protruding end of the shank (shin) bone, positioning it with the rounded, meaty side up and tilting it upward. Then, with a sharp knife, thinly slice the meat, cutting away from you and almost parallel to the bone.

2 Rotate the leg to reveal the long muscle on the opposite side, then carve into thin slices.

3 Finally, carve the meat from the shank end, parallel to the bone and close to where the leg is held. As you work, arrange the meat, slightly overlapping the slices, on a serving platter.

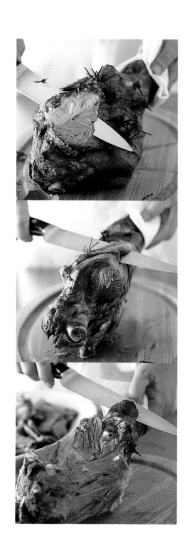

14

Stuffing and trussing poultry

1 Rinse the inside and outside of the bird, here a chicken, with cold running water and dry thoroughly with paper towels.

2 Spoon the stuffing into the body cavity, being careful not to pack it tightly.

3 Cut a length of kitchen string about twice the length of the bird. Tuck each wing tip under the back of the bird, and place the bird on its back. Slip the string under the wings, securing the wing tips to the body.

4 Cross the string over the center of the back of the bird, then bring the ends under the drumsticks, returning the ends to the breast side.

5 Tie the drumsticks together, wrap the string around the tail, pull tightly, and tie to secure. Trim any excess string.

Carving a turkey

1 Lay the cooked turkey, breast side up, on a carving board. If it is stuffed, remove the stuffing from the cavity. Using a sharp knife, cut off the leg and thigh from each side of the body by cutting through the hip joint.

2 Separate the thighs from the drumsticks by cutting through the joint.

3 Cutting parallel to the bone, slice the meat from the drumsticks and thighs.

4 Move a wing to locate the joint to the body, then cut off the wing. Cut off the other wing in the same way.

5 To carve the breast meat, make a horizontal base cut just above the wing and thigh joints toward the bone. Then, starting at the breastbone, cut downward to create thin slices, stopping at the base cut.

Deglazing and making a pan sauce or gravy

1   Pour off the excess fat from the roasting pan. Alternatively, pour the pan drippings—fat and juices—into a clear glass pitcher, let stand for a minute or so, and then spoon off the fat that rises to the surface. Reserve the fat and return the defatted juices to the pan.

2   Place the pan over high heat on the stove top. Add a splash of wine or stock, bring to a boil, and scrape the base of the pan with a wooden spoon to dislodge any browned-on bits. If making pan sauce, add more liquid, if recipe indicates, then reduce until slightly thickened. Season with salt and pepper and strain through a sieve into a warmed bowl.

3   If making gravy, remove all but about 1 tablespoon fat from drippings in step 1. Deglaze the pan with a splash of liquid as directed in step 2, then sprinkle in about 1 tablespoon flour and stir rapidly to blend the flour smoothly into the liquid.

4   When the liquid is absorbed and the pan mixture begins to boil, pour in the remaining liquid, whisk to combine, and then simmer, stirring, until slightly thickened.

5   Season gravy with salt and pepper and strain through a sieve into a warmed bowl.

Cooking guide

See pages 10–11 for directions on testing for doneness and page 12 for information on thermometers.

Beef and veal

Rare 140°F (60°C)

Medium-rare 150°F (65°C)

Medium 155°F (70°C)

Well-done 165°F (75°C)

Lamb

Medium-rare 140°F (60°C)

Medium 150°F (65°C)

Well-done 175°F (80°C)

Pork

Medium 155°F (70°C)

Chicken, turkey, and duck

155°F (70°C) for chicken breast, 175°F (80°C) for chicken thigh

165°F (75°C) for turkey breast, 175°F (80°C) for turkey thigh

150°F (65°C) for duck breast, 175°F (80°C) for duck thigh

Alternatively, insert a thin skewer into the thigh joint; the juices should run clear.

Fish

Using the tip of a knife or a fork, test that flesh is opaque throughout, is moist, and flakes easily from the bone.

Marinades and rubs

Lemon and rosemary marinade

Use this marinade for chicken, turkey, pork, lamb, duck, fish, or vegetables.

1 lemon
¼ cup (2 fl. oz./60 ml) fresh lemon juice
½ cup (4 fl. oz./125 ml) olive oil
Leaves from 4 fresh rosemary sprigs
5 cloves garlic
Sea salt and freshly ground black pepper

Using vegetable peeler, remove lemon zest in narrow strips, allowing them to fall into large, nonreactive bowl. Add lemon juice and olive oil. In mortar, combine rosemary leaves and garlic cloves and roughly bruise leaves and crush garlic with pestle. Add to bowl holding olive oil and lemon, stir well, and season with salt and pepper.

Add item to be roasted, turn to coat evenly, cover, and refrigerate for 3 hours for fish, or at least 3 hours or up to 24 hours for other items.

Makes 1 cup (8 fl. oz./250 ml), enough marinade for about 3 lb. (1.5 kg)

Red-wine marinade

Use this marinade for beef, veal, pork, lamb, or duck.

1 orange
1 yellow (brown) onion, thinly sliced
2 carrots, peeled and roughly chopped
3 celery stalks, roughly chopped
3 bay leaves
8 black peppercorns
5 juniper berries
6 cups (48 fl. oz./1.5 L) red wine
3 tablespoons olive oil
Sea salt

Using vegetable peeler, remove orange zest in narrow strips, allowing them to fall into a large, nonreactive bowl. Add onion, carrots, celery, bay leaves, peppercorns, and juniper berries. Pour in wine and olive oil, stir well to combine, season with salt, and stir again.

Add item to be roasted, turn to coat evenly, cover, and refrigerate for at least 6 hours or overnight.

Makes 10 cups (80 fl. oz./2.5 L), enough marinade for about 4 lb. (2 kg)

Southeast Asian marinade

Use this marinade for fish, chicken, pork, or vegetables.

3–4 limes, about 10 oz. (300 g)

2 tablespoons superfine (caster) sugar

¼ cup (2 fl. oz./60 ml) fish sauce (see note)

3 cloves garlic, thinly sliced

2 long, red fresh chilies, thinly sliced

¼ cup (2 oz./60 g) peeled and thinly sliced fresh ginger

1 bunch fresh cilantro (fresh coriander), preferably with roots intact

Juice limes, placing juice in large, nonreactive bowl and reserving the rinds. Add sugar to lime juice and stir until sugar dissolves. Add fish sauce, garlic, chilies, ginger, and reserved lime rinds. Roughly chop cilantro, including stems and roots, add to bowl, and stir well.

Add item to be roasted, turn to coat evenly, cover, and refrigerate for 3 hours for fish, or at least 3 hours or up to 24 hours for other items.

Makes 4 cups (32 fl. oz./1 L), enough marinade for about 3 lb. (1.5 kg)

Note: Fish sauce is a common southeast Asian condiment made by layering small, anchovy-like fish and salt in wooden barrels, leaving them to ferment, and then pressing to extract the salty, pungent liquid. Look for Vietnamese or Thai brands.

Middle Eastern rub

Use this rub for chicken, lamb, fish, or vegetables.

1 cinnamon stick, broken into small pieces

8 black peppercorns

4 whole allspice

5 cardamom pods

1 tablespoon cumin seeds

1 tablespoon coriander seeds

Sea salt

Olive oil for coating

In frying pan, combine cinnamon, peppercorns, allspice, and cardamom over medium heat. Toast, stirring occasionally, for 3 minutes. Add cumin and coriander and continue to toast until all spices are aromatic, about 2 minutes longer. Remove from heat, pour onto small plate, and set aside to cool for 10 minutes.

Pour spices into mortar and grind finely with pestle. Season with salt and stir to mix.

Lightly coat item to be roasted with oil. Sprinkle evenly with seasoning mixture, then rub in or toss to combine evenly.

Makes 3 tablespoons, enough rub for about 4 lb. (2 kg)

Indian spice rub or marinade

Use this rub or marinade for chicken, turkey, pork, lamb, veal, duck, fish, or vegetables.

2 teaspoons black mustard seeds (see glossary)
2 teaspoons coriander seeds
1 teaspoon cumin seeds
1 teaspoon fenugreek seeds (see glossary)
4 cardamom pods
1 cinnamon stick, broken into small pieces
1 teaspoon ground ginger
$1/2$ teaspoon ground turmeric
Canola oil for coating (optional)
Plain (natural) yogurt (optional)

In frying pan, toast mustard seeds over medium heat, stirring often, until they begin to pop, about 6 minutes. Pour onto plate and set aside to cool. Meanwhile, in same pan, combine coriander, cumin, fenugreek, cardamom, and cinnamon stick over medium heat and toast, stirring often, until aromatic, about 3 minutes. Remove from heat, pour onto another small plate, and set aside to cool for 10 minutes.

Pour toasted spices into mortar and finely crush with pestle. Stir in ginger and turmeric.

Lightly coat item to be roasted with oil. Sprinkle evenly with seasoning mixture, then rub in or toss to combine evenly. Alternatively, omit oil and stir seasoning mixture into plain yogurt to form a marinade, using a ratio of 1 teaspoon seasoning mixture to 1 cup (8 oz./250 g) yogurt.

Makes 3 tablespoons, enough rub for about 4 lb. (2 kg); 1 cup seasoned yogurt makes enough marinade for about 2 lb. (1 kg)

Mediterranean rub

Use this rub for chicken, pork, lamb, fish, or vegetables.

1 tablespoon fennel seeds
3 bay leaves
2 cloves garlic
$1/4$ cup ($1/4$ oz./7 g) fresh marjoram leaves, roughly
  chopped
Grated zest of 1 lemon
Sea salt and freshly ground black pepper
Olive oil for coating

In mortar, combine fennel seeds, bay leaves, and garlic and crush together roughly with pestle. Transfer to small, nonreactive bowl. Add marjoram leaves and lemon zest, stir to mix, season with salt and pepper, and stir again.

Lightly coat item to be roasted with oil. Sprinkle evenly with seasoning mixture, then rub in or toss to combine evenly.

Makes 3 tablespoons, enough rub for about 4 lb. (2 kg)

Stuffings

Bread and herb stuffing

Use this stuffing for chicken, turkey, pork, lamb, duck, or fish.

6 tablespoons (3 oz./90 g) butter
1 yellow (brown) onion, finely chopped
6 oz./180 g regular sliced bacon, roughly chopped
3$\frac{1}{2}$ cups (6$\frac{1}{2}$ oz./200 g) fresh bread crumbs
2 tablespoons fresh sage leaves, roughly chopped, or
    2 teaspoons dried sage
2 tablespoons fresh thyme leaves or 2 teaspoons dried
    thyme
2 tablespoons fresh oregano leaves or 2 teaspoons
    dried oregano
Salt and freshly ground black pepper

In large frying pan, melt butter over medium-high heat. Add onion and bacon and cook, stirring occasionally, until onion is translucent and bacon is crisp, about 5 minutes. Remove from heat.

In large bowl, combine bread crumbs, sage, thyme, and oregano. Add the onion mixture, season with salt and pepper, and mix until well combined, as pictured page 25.

Makes about 4 cups (14 oz./460 g)

Couscous stuffing

Use this stuffing for chicken, turkey, pork, or lamb.

2 tablespoons olive oil
1 yellow (brown) onion, halved and thinly sliced
2 teaspoons ground cumin
2 teaspoons ground coriander
1 teaspoon ground cinnamon
1 teaspoon ground ginger
1 tablespoon honey
2 cups (10 oz./300 g) instant couscous
1$\frac{1}{2}$ cups (12 fl. oz./375 ml) boiling water
1 rounded cup (6$\frac{1}{2}$ oz./200 g) fresh or dried dates,
    pitted and roughly chopped
$\frac{1}{2}$ cup (2 oz./60 g) pistachio nuts
2 cups (2 oz./60 g) fresh cilantro (fresh coriander)
    leaves
Salt and freshly ground black pepper

In large frying pan, heat oil over medium heat. Add onion and cook, stirring occasionally, until dark golden brown, about 15 minutes. Add cumin, coriander, cinnamon, ginger, and honey and stir to combine. Remove from heat and set aside for 15 minutes to cool.

Place couscous in large, heatproof bowl and pour in boiling water. Cover with plastic wrap and set aside for 5 minutes.

Uncover couscous and fluff grains with a fork. Add onion mixture, dates, pistachios, cilantro, and some salt and pepper, and stir gently to distribute all ingredients evenly.

Makes about 3 cups (1$\frac{1}{4}$ lb./625 g)

24

Ricotta cheese stuffing

Use this stuffing for chicken, turkey, pork, or duck.

2 cups (1 lb./500 g) ricotta cheese
1/2 cup (1/2 oz./15 g) fresh mint leaves, roughly chopped
1/2 cup (1/2 oz./15 g) flat-leaf (Italian) parsley leaves,
  roughly chopped
1/3 cup (1/3 oz./10 g) fresh basil leaves, roughly chopped
2 tablespoons fresh sage leaves, roughly chopped
2 tablespoons fresh thyme leaves, roughly chopped
1 egg
Salt and freshly ground black pepper

In large bowl, place ricotta cheese and mash with fork until
soft. Add mint, parsley, basil, sage, thyme, egg, and a little
salt and pepper and mix until well combined.

Makes about 2¹/₂ cups (18 oz./560 g)

Sauces and accompaniments

Bread and watercress sauce

Serve with chicken or turkey.

3 cups (24 fl. oz./750 ml) milk
6 whole cloves
1 yellow (brown) onion, halved
1/2 cup (2 oz./60 g) fine bread crumbs from day-old
    bread
2 tablespoons butter (1 oz./30 g)
1/4 teaspoon ground nutmeg
1/4 lb./125 g finely chopped watercress sprigs, about
    4 cups, tough stems removed
Salt and freshly ground black pepper

In saucepan, heat milk over low heat. Press 3 cloves into each onion half and place onion halves in the milk. When milk comes to boil, remove and discard onion halves. Add bread crumbs to boiling milk, whisking until sauce is thick and most of milk has been absorbed. Remove from heat, add butter and nutmeg, and stir until combined. Add watercress, stir to mix, and season with salt and pepper. Remove from heat, let cool, and serve at room temperature.

Makes about 3 1/4 cups (26 fl. oz./800 ml)

Piri piri sauce

Serve with chicken, turkey, or pork.

3 fresh, long, red chili peppers
1 red bell pepper (capsicum)
3 cloves garlic
1 cup (8 fl. oz./250 ml) olive oil
1 egg yolk
Salt and freshly ground black pepper

Preheat oven to 350°F (180°C/Gas 4). Place chili peppers, bell pepper, and garlic on rimmed baking sheet and drizzle with 1 tablespoon oil. Place in oven and roast until skins of the chili peppers and bell pepper have blackened and garlic is lightly browned, about 30 minutes. Remove from oven and place chili peppers and bell pepper in plastic bag. Seal bag and set aside for 10 minutes to cool. Let garlic cool to the touch.

  Peel chili peppers, bell pepper, and garlic, and remove seeds from bell pepper. In a food processor, combine peeled vegetables and process until smooth. Add egg yolk and process until pale and frothy. With motor running, add remaining oil in slow, steady stream until thickened to mayonnaise-like consistency. Season with salt and pepper. Cover and refrigerate until serving.

Makes about 1 3/4 cups (14 fl. oz./450 ml)

Note: Eating raw or undercooked chicken eggs should be avoided in areas where salmonella has been a problem. Although not foolproof, purchasing eggs from free-range hens raised on organic feed is recommended.

Applesauce

Serve with pork, turkey, duck, or chicken.

1½ lb. (750 g) green apples, about 4–5 medium, peeled,
    cored, and roughly chopped
1¾ cups (14 fl. oz./440 ml) water
1 tablespoon fresh lemon juice
1 cinnamon stick or ½ teaspoon ground cinnamon
½ cup (4 oz./125 g) sugar
Salt and freshly ground black pepper

In saucepan, combine apples, water, lemon juice, and cinnamon stick or ground cinnamon over high heat and bring to boil. Cook uncovered, stirring occasionally, until apples break down and are smooth, about 20 minutes. Remove cinnamon stick, if using, and discard. Add sugar, stir well, and season with salt and pepper. Reduce heat to medium and continue to cook, stirring occasionally, until sugar dissolves, about 5 minutes. Remove from heat and serve hot, or let cool and serve at room temperature.

Makes about 3¼ cups (26 fl. oz./800 ml)

Cranberry sauce

Serve with turkey.

1 cup (4 oz./125 g) dried cranberries
1¼ cups (10 fl. oz./300 ml) water
¼ cup (2 oz./60 g) superfine (caster) sugar

In a saucepan, combine cranberries and water over high heat and bring to boil. Reduce the heat to medium and simmer cranberries until softened, about 15 minutes. Add sugar and continue to cook, uncovered, until sugar dissolves and liquid thickens to light syrup, about 5 minutes. Remove from heat and serve hot or at room temperature.

Makes about 1¼ cups (10 fl. oz./300 ml)

Mint sauce

The perfect accompaniment to lamb.

1 cup (1 oz./30 g) fresh mint leaves
2 teaspoons superfine (caster) sugar
¼ cup (2 fl. oz./60 ml) boiling water
2 tablespoons white-wine vinegar

In mortar, roughly crush mint leaves with a pestle. Add sugar and continue to pound until nearly smooth. Add boiling water and vinegar and stir to combine. Serve immediately, as sauce will darken if left to stand.

Makes about ¾ cup (6 fl. oz./180 ml)

Pickled cherries

Serve with chicken, pork, duck, turkey, sausages, or any cured meats.

3 cups (24 fl. oz./750 ml) white-wine vinegar
$^3/_4$ cup plus 2 tablespoons (7 oz./220 g) sugar
6 black peppercorns
4 whole cloves
3 bay leaves
1 cinnamon stick
$1^1/_3$ lb. (650 g) cherries, about 4 cups

In large, nonreactive saucepan, combine vinegar, sugar, peppercorns, cloves, bay leaves, and cinnamon stick. Place over medium-high heat and bring to simmer, stirring until sugar dissolves. Simmer mixture, uncovered, for 10 minutes to blend flavors, then remove from heat. Set aside for 10 minutes to cool slightly.

Place cherries in one or more cool, sterilized jars and pour in vinegar-sugar mixture to cover. Seal with lids and invert jars for 5 minutes to create vacuum. Turn upright and let cool to room temperature. Store in cool, dry place. To allow flavor to mellow, do not open for two weeks; cherries will keep for up to 6 months. Once opened, store in refrigerator.

Makes about 2 cups (1 pt/500 ml)

Crème anglaise

Serve with puddings, pies, and poached fruits.

1 vanilla bean, halved lengthwise
2 cups (16 fl. oz./500 ml) milk
1 cup (8 fl. oz./250 ml) light (single) cream
6 egg yolks
$^2/_3$ cup (4 oz./125 g) superfine (caster) sugar

Using knife tip, remove seeds from vanilla bean halves and add seeds and pods to a saucepan. Add milk and cream, place over medium heat, and bring to a boil. Meanwhile, in bowl, combine egg yolks and sugar. Using balloon whisk, beat until pale and frothy.

When milk mixture is at boil, remove from heat. Gradually pour hot milk mixture into egg yolk mixture, whisking constantly until combined. Then pour yolk-milk mixture into saucepan, return to low heat, and cook uncovered, stirring constantly with wooden spoon until the mixture thickens enough to coat back of spoon, about 10–15 minutes. Strain through fine-mesh sieve into bowl to remove lumps. Serve immediately or cover with plastic wrap pressed directly on surface (to prevent skin from forming), refrigerate for up to 24 hours, and serve cold.

Makes about $3^1/_2$ cups (28 fl. oz./875 ml)

Tip: This cooled sauce can be put into an ice-cream maker and, following the manufacturer's directions, churned to create vanilla ice cream.

Candied kumquats

The acidity of kumquats makes them the perfect accompaniment for the richness of duck and pork.

2 lb. (1 kg) kumquats
6 cups (3 lb./1.5 kg) sugar
6 cups (48 fl. oz./1.5 l) water

Using serrated knife, halve kumquats lengthwise and remove seeds. In large, nonreactive saucepan, combine sugar and water over medium heat and stir until sugar dissolves. Raise heat to high, bring to a boil, and boil for 5 minutes. Add kumquats, reduce heat to medium, and simmer gently, uncovered, until softened, about 5 minutes.

Spoon kumquats and syrup into sterilized jars, seal with lids, and invert jars for 5 minutes to create vacuum. Turn upright and let cool to room temperature. Store in cool, dry place for up to 3 months. Once opened, store in refrigerator.

Makes about 2¹/₂ cups (1¹/₄ pt/625 ml)

Pralines

Sprinkle ground pralines on roasted fruit or stir into Crème Anglaise (page 28). Serve pieces with Rhubarb and Strawberries with Rose Water (page 100).

³/₄ cup plus 2 tablespoons (7 oz./220 g) sugar
3 tablespoons water
¹/₂ cup (2 oz./60 g) slivered blanched almonds

Grease rimmed baking sheet or line with parchment (baking) paper. In saucepan with light-colored interior (to judge color of caramel more easily), combine sugar and water over medium heat and cook, stirring constantly, until sugar dissolves. Raise heat to high and bring to boil. Let syrup cook, uncovered and without stirring, until golden brown (hard-crack stage, or 300°F/150°C on candy thermometer), about 10 minutes. Do not let it darken too much, or it will taste burned. If necessary, while syrup boils, brush down any crystals that form on pan sides with pastry brush dipped in hot water. Remove from heat, add the almonds, and swirl the pan to distribute evenly. Pour hot caramel onto prepared baking sheet; it will spread naturally. Set aside to cool completely.

To serve, break into rough pieces or grind to desired consistency in food processor.

Makes about 1¹/₂ cups (8 oz./250 g)

Beef and veal

Beef top round stuffed with basil and pine nuts

1 piece beef top round (topside), about 4 lb. (2 kg) and
   6 inches (15 cm) thick

2 cups (2 oz./60 g) fresh basil leaves

2 cups (4 oz./125 g) sourdough or plain fresh bread
   crumbs

1/4 cup (1 oz./30 g) pine nuts

1 yellow (brown) onion, chopped

6 fresh sage leaves, finely chopped

Salt and freshly ground black pepper

2–3 tablespoons milk

Olive oil for brushing

4 heads garlic, halved crosswise

Ask your butcher to butterfly beef round. Alternatively, butterfly it yourself: start at narrow side, and using large, sharp knife, cut to within about 1/2 inch (12 mm) of opposite side. Lay meat flat, cut side up, on work surface. Arrange basil leaves evenly over meat. In bowl, combine bread crumbs, pine nuts, onion, sage, and a little salt and pepper, and mix well. Gradually pour in milk while stirring constantly, adding only enough to bind ingredients together. Spread the mixture evenly over basil leaves.

Starting from long side, roll up meat into cylinder, then secure in place with dampened kitchen string at 3-inch (7.5-cm) intervals along length of roll. Brush entire surface with oil.

Preheat oven to 350ºF (180ºC/Gas 4). Place beef roll on greased flat roasting rack in roasting pan. Add garlic to pan. Place beef in oven and roast until a thermometer inserted into thickest part registers 155ºF (70ºC) for medium, about 1 1/4 hours, or 165ºF (75ºC) for well done, about 1 hour and 25 minutes. Remove meat to carving board, cover loosely with aluminum foil, and let rest for 15 minutes before carving.

Snip the strings, carve meat into thick slices, and arrange on warmed plates. You can also let meat cool completely before carving, then slice and serve at room temperature. Serve 1/2 head garlic alongside each serving for smearing on the meat.

Serves 8

Beef sirloin roast with red-wine gravy and Yorkshire puddings

1 boneless beef sirloin roast, 4 lb. (2 kg)

Salt and freshly ground black pepper

3 tablespoons olive oil

1/4 cup (2 fl. oz./60 ml) dry red wine

1 tablespoon all-purpose (plain) flour

1 1/4 cups (10 fl. oz./300 ml) beef stock

1/2 cup (4 fl. oz./125 ml) prepared horseradish (horseradish cream)

Yorkshire Puddings

Reserved fat from pan, plus canola oil if needed

3/4 cup (4 oz./125 g) all-purpose (plain) flour

1/2 teaspoon salt

2 eggs

1 1/4 cups (10 fl. oz./300 ml) milk

Preheat oven to 425°F (220°C/Gas 7). Place roast, fat side up, in roasting pan. Season well with salt and pepper, then drizzle with olive oil. Rub salt, pepper, and olive oil evenly over meat.

Place beef in oven and roast for 15 minutes. Reduce oven temperature to 350°F (180°C/Gas 4) and continue to roast until a thermometer inserted into the thickest part registers 150°F (65°C) for medium-rare, 40–45 minutes longer, or 155°F (70°C) for medium, about 50 minutes longer. Remove beef to carving board, cover loosely with aluminum foil, and let rest for 15 minutes before carving.

Pour contents of pan into clear glass measuring pitcher, let stand for a minute or so, and then spoon off all but about 1 tablespoon fat from the surface. Reserve removed fat for making Yorkshire puddings. Return defatted drippings to pan and set aside. Alternatively, pour off excess fat from roasting pan, leaving about 1 tablespoon behind.

To make Yorkshire puddings: Increase oven temperature to 400°F (200°C/Gas 6). Pour 1 tablespoon of reserved fat into each of 6 muffin-pan cups. If there is too little fat, use canola oil to make up difference. Place pan in oven to heat. In large bowl, sift together flour and salt. Add eggs and whisk to combine. Add milk in thin, steady stream, whisking constantly to form smooth batter. Remove pan from oven, divide batter evenly among muffin cups, and return to oven. Bake puddings until puffed and golden, about 20 minutes.

Meanwhile, make gravy: Place roasting pan over medium heat on stove top. Add 1 tablespoon wine, bring to simmer, and deglaze pan, using wooden spoon to scrape up any browned-on bits from pan bottom. Sprinkle in flour and stir rapidly to blend flour smoothly into liquid. Cook until liquid is absorbed and mixture begins to boil, about 2 minutes. Gradually pour in stock and remaining 3 tablespoons wine, stirring between additions to incorporate fully. When all liquid has been added, continue to simmer, stirring constantly, until slightly thickened, about 2 minutes. Strain gravy through fine-mesh sieve into warmed bowl (or pitcher for easier pouring).

Just before puddings are ready, carve beef into thin slices and arrange on warmed dinner plates. Accompany each serving with a Yorkshire pudding. Pour gravy over beef and puddings and serve a spoonful of horseradish alongside each serving.

Serves 6

Rack of veal stuffed with olives and marjoram

Serve with Mixed Spring Vegetables (page 91).

1 rack of veal, about 2³/₄ lb. (1.3 kg), with 8 ribs, frenched

¹/₃ cup (2 oz./60 g) pitted Kalamata olives, roughly chopped

¹/₃ cup (2 oz./60 g) pitted green olives, roughly chopped

2 tablespoons fresh marjoram leaves, roughly chopped

Salt and freshly ground black pepper

10 thin slices pancetta

2 tablespoons olive oil

Ask your butcher to french veal rack for you. Alternatively, do it yourself: Using a sharp knife, cut away all meat and tissue from upper 2–3 inches (5–7.5 cm) of bones. Trim any excess fat from veal rack. Then, using long, thin, sharp knife, cut 1-inch (2.5-cm) slit, or tunnel, lengthwise through center of veal rack. Set rack aside.

In bowl, combine Kalamata and green olives, marjoram, and a little salt and pepper (use caution, as olives can be salty) and stir to combine. Press olive mixture into slit in veal rack, making sure it is spread along its length. Season veal rack with salt and pepper. Lay pancetta slices, overlapping them slightly, over meaty portion of rack, then secure in place by tying with dampened kitchen string between each pair of bones.

Preheat oven to 350°F (180°C/Gas 4). Place veal rack in roasting pan and drizzle with oil. Place veal in oven and roast until thermometer inserted into thickest part away from bone registers 155°F (70°C) for medium, about 50 minutes. Remove meat from oven, cover loosely with aluminum foil, and let rest for 15 minutes before carving.

Snip strings and carve rack into individual ribs. Arrange 2 rib chops, along with crisp pancetta, on each warmed plate and serve.

Serves 4

Short ribs with orange-and-wasabi glaze

Orange-and-wasabi glaze
1 cup (8 fl. oz./250 ml) fresh orange juice
1/2 cup (4 oz./125 g) sugar
2 teaspoons fish sauce (see note, page 22)
Zest of 1 orange, cut into narrow strips
1 tablespoon wasabi paste (see note)

4 lb. (2 kg) beef short ribs, in 2 portions
2 tablespoons sesame seeds
1 cup (6 1/2 oz./200 g) jasmine rice (see note)
1 1/2 cups (12 fl. oz./375 ml) water
1/2 cup (1/2 oz./15 g) fresh cilantro
   (fresh coriander) leaves

To make orange-and-wasabi glaze: In saucepan, combine orange juice and sugar over high heat. Bring to boil, stirring to dissolve sugar, then reduce heat to medium and cook, stirring occasionally, until mixture thickens slightly, 3–5 minutes. Remove from heat, add fish sauce and orange zest, stir well, and let cool to room temperature.

Preheat oven to 375°F (190°C/Gas 5). Place beef ribs in roasting pan just large enough to accommodate them. Divide wasabi paste between beef ribs and evenly rub into meat. Drizzle meat evenly with orange glaze. Place ribs in oven and roast, basting occasionally with pan drippings, until nicely browned, about 20 minutes. Reduce oven temperature to 300°F (150°C/Gas 2) and continue roasting, basting occasionally, until meat is tender and comes away from bone easily, about 2 hours longer.

Meanwhile, in small frying pan, toast sesame seeds over medium heat, stirring occasionally, until golden brown, about 6 minutes. Pour onto plate to cool.

Place rice in sieve and rinse under cold running water until water runs clear. Put rinsed rice in saucepan, add water, and place on stove top over high heat. Bring to boil, cover, reduce heat to low, and cook until all water is absorbed and rice is tender, 8–10 minutes after reducing heat. Remove from heat, add cilantro, and stir to distribute evenly.

Remove beef from oven. Cut ribs apart and arrange on warmed platter. Sprinkle sesame seeds over ribs and serve with rice.

Serves 4

Note: Wasabi, a spicy root similar to horseradish, is a popular Japanese ingredient. It is sold powdered in small cans and as a paste in tubes. Jasmine rice is a naturally fragrant long-grain white rice grown primarily in Thailand. Cooking time can vary by brand. Both products are sold in Asian markets and well-stocked grocery stores.

Red wine-marinated beef tenderloin with balsamic-glazed onion

1 beef tenderloin (fillet), 3 lb. (1½ kg)
Red Wine Marinade (page 20)
2 lb. (1 kg) small white boiling (pickling) onions, each
   1–1½ inches (2.5–4 cm) in diameter
2 tablespoons olive oil
Salt and freshly ground black pepper
1 tablespoon superfine (caster) sugar
¼ cup (2 fl. oz./60 ml) balsamic vinegar
7 oz. (220 g) baby arugula (rocket) leaves
Potato Stacks (Potatoes Anna) (page 93)

Trim any excess fat from beef tenderloin. Fold tail of tenderloin under to create even shape and thickness, and tie at 2-inch (5-cm) intervals with dampened kitchen string. Place beef in nonreactive container just large enough to accommodate it, and pour the marinade over the top. Turn to coat, then cover and refrigerate for at least 3 hours or up to 3 days.

Preheat oven to 400°F (200°C/Gas 6). Arrange onions in single layer on rimmed baking sheet. Pour 1 tablespoon oil over onions, season with salt and pepper, and toss to coat evenly. Remove beef from marinade, pat thoroughly dry with paper towels, and place in pan with onions. Drizzle beef with remaining 1 tablespoon oil, and season with salt and pepper.

Place beef in oven and roast until thermometer inserted into thickest part registers 150°F (65°C) for medium-rare, or meat springs back when pressed with fingertip, about 40 minutes. Remove beef to carving board, cover loosely with aluminum foil, and let rest for 15 minutes before carving.

In small bowl, stir together sugar and vinegar until sugar dissolves. Pour over onions and turn to coat evenly. Return onions to oven and continue cooking, stirring occasionally, until syrup is reduced and onions are tender, about 10 minutes longer.

Carve beef across grain into thin slices. Serve with onions, arugula, and potatoes.

Serves 8

Lamb

Slow-roasted lamb shoulder with tarragon and flageolet beans

1 bone-in lamb shoulder, 3$\frac{1}{2}$ lb. (1.75 kg)

6 anchovy fillets packed in olive oil

6 tablespoons (3 fl. oz./90 ml) olive oil

Salt and freshly ground black pepper

1 lemon

$\frac{1}{2}$ cup ($\frac{1}{2}$ oz./15 g) fresh tarragon leaves, roughly
  chopped

3 shallots (French shallots), finely chopped

1 cup (7 oz./220 g) dried flageolet beans or small green
  lima beans, soaked overnight in water to cover and
  drained

1 tablespoon Dijon mustard

Preheat oven to 350°F (180°C/Gas 4). Using sharp knife, cut 6 slits, each $^3/_4$ inch (2 cm) deep, evenly over surface of lamb. Cut 3 anchovy fillets in half, and place half an anchovy fillet into each slit. Place lamb in roasting pan, drizzle with 2 tablespoons oil, and season with salt and pepper. Rub oil and seasonings into lamb.

Place lamb in oven and roast for 30 minutes. Reduce heat to 300°F (150°C/Gas 2) and continue roasting until meat comes easily away from the bone, about 1 hour longer.

While lamb roasts, in small bowl, grate zest from lemon and set lemon aside. Roughly chop remaining anchovies and add to zest along with tarragon and shallots. Stir to combine and set aside.

Fill large saucepan with salted water and bring to boil over high heat. Add drained beans, reduce heat to medium, and cook, uncovered, until tender, about 1 hour and 20 minutes. Drain beans into colander, then transfer to bowl. Squeeze juice from reserved lemon and measure out 1 tablespoon into small bowl. Add mustard and remaining 4 tablespoons oil and stir to mix. Season with salt and pepper, then stir mixture through warm beans; keep warm.

Remove lamb to carving board, cover loosely with aluminum foil, and let rest for 5 minutes.

Carve lamb. Spoon beans onto warmed dinner plates, dividing evenly, and top with lamb. Sprinkle tarragon over top and serve.

Serves 4

Leg of lamb with vegetables and mint sauce

1 bone-in leg of lamb, 4 lb. (2 kg)

4 cloves garlic, thinly sliced

Leaves from 2 fresh rosemary sprigs

2 lb. (1 kg) potatoes, about 7 medium, peeled and
quartered

3 tablespoons olive oil

Salt and freshly ground black pepper

1 butternut squash (pumpkin), 1½ lb. (750 g), halved,
seeded, peeled, and cut into 2-inch (5-cm) pieces

1½ lb. (750 g) rutabagas (swedes), about 1–2, peeled
and cut into 2-inch (5-cm) pieces

10 oz. (300 g) carrots, about 3 medium, peeled and cut
into 2-inch (5-cm) lengths

1 lb. (500 g) red onions, about 3 medium, quartered
through stem end

½ cup (4 fl. oz./125 ml) dry red wine

1 tablespoon all-purpose (plain) flour

½ cup (4 fl. oz./125 ml) chicken stock

Mint Sauce (page 27)

Position one oven rack in lower third of oven and another oven rack in upper third of oven and preheat to 400ºF (200ºC/Gas 6). Trim excess fat from lamb leg. Using paring knife, cut slits ³/₄ inch (2 cm) deep evenly over surface of lamb. Slip garlic slices and rosemary leaves into slits. Place lamb in roasting pan and arrange potatoes around lamb. Drizzle lamb and potatoes with 2 tablespoons oil, season with salt and pepper, and then rub oil, salt, and pepper evenly over lamb.

In roasting pan large enough to hold vegetables in single layer, combine squash, rutabagas, and carrots. Drizzle with remaining 1 tablespoon oil, season with salt and pepper, toss to coat evenly, and spread out evenly.

Place lamb on upper oven rack and vegetables on lower rack. Roast lamb and vegetables for 15 minutes. Add onions to pan holding vegetables, reduce heat to 350ºF (180ºC/Gas 4), and continue roasting until thermometer inserted into lamb at thickest part away from bone registers 150ºF (65ºC) for medium, about 1 hour and 10 minutes longer. Transfer lamb to carving board, cover loosely with aluminum foil, and let rest for 15 minutes before carving.

Remove potatoes from pan and add to other vegetables. Return vegetables to lower rack in oven and continue to roast until golden brown and tender, about 15 minutes longer.

Meanwhile, make gravy: Pour pan drippings from lamb into clear glass measuring pitcher, let stand for a minute or so, and then spoon off all but about 1 tablespoon fat from surface. Return defatted drippings to pan. Alternatively, pour off excess fat from roasting pan, leaving about 1 tablespoon behind. Place pan over high heat on stove top. Add wine, bring to boil, and deglaze pan, using wooden spoon to dislodge any browned-on bits from pan bottom. Sprinkle in flour and stir rapidly to blend flour smoothly into liquid. Cook until liquid is

absorbed and mixture begins to boil, about 2 minutes. Gradually pour in stock, stirring between additions to incorporate fully. When all stock has been added, continue to simmer, stirring constantly, until slightly thickened, about 2 minutes. Strain gravy through fine-mesh sieve into warmed bowl.

Carve lamb as directed on page 14. Serve with vegetables, gravy, and mint sauce.

Serves 6

Variations

For lighter gravy, substitute dry white wine for red wine. Or, for nonalcoholic version, substitute apple juice for wine.

For rosemary-flavored gravy, add 2 teaspoons chopped fresh rosemary to pan before placing on stove top.

For sweeter gravy, stir 1 tablespoon cranberry jelly into gravy just before serving.

Cinnamon-spiced rack of lamb with sumac-roasted tomatoes

6 racks of lamb, each with 4 ribs and about
   ³/₄ lb. (375 g), frenched
1 tablespoon ground cinnamon
Sea salt and freshly ground black pepper
4 tablespoons (2 fl. oz./60 ml) olive oil
6 plum (Roma) tomatoes
6 Japanese eggplants (aubergines)
2 teaspoons ground sumac (see note)
¹/₃ cup (3¹/₂ oz./100 g) plain (natural) yogurt
¹/₄ cup (¹/₄ oz./7 g) fresh mint leaves, finely chopped
3¹/₂ oz. (100 g) baby spinach leaves
¹/₄ cup (1 oz./30 g) pine nuts, toasted

Preheat oven to 350°F (180°C/Gas 4). Ask your butcher to french lamb racks for you. Alternatively, do it yourself: Using a sharp knife, cut away all meat and tissue from upper 2 inches (5 cm) of bones. Trim any excess fat from lamb racks. Sprinkle meaty portions of lamb racks with cinnamon, season with salt and pepper, and drizzle with 2 tablespoons oil. Rub oil and seasonings into lamb, then place in large roasting pan.

Halve tomatoes and eggplants lengthwise and lay them, skin side down, in roasting pan around lamb racks. Drizzle tomatoes and eggplants with remaining 2 tablespoons olive oil and sprinkle tomatoes with sumac.

Place lamb in oven and roast until thermometer inserted into thickest part away from bone registers 140°F (60°C) for medium-rare, about 20 minutes. Remove lamb to carving board, cover loosely with aluminum foil, and let rest for 5 minutes.

Meanwhile, return vegetables to oven until tender, about 5 minutes. In small bowl, stir together yogurt and mint.

Cut racks into individual rib chops and arrange 4 chops on each warmed dinner plate. Accompany with spinach leaves and a spoonful of minted yogurt sprinkled with pine nuts.

Serves 6

Note: Sumac, the dried and ground deep-red berries of a vine, lends a fruity, distinctive seasoning to many dishes in the Middle East. Look for it in Middle Eastern markets.

Lamb and spring vegetable salad

³/₄ lb. (375 g) boneless lamb loin

Salt and freshly ground black pepper

¹/₄ **cup (2 fl. oz./60 ml) olive oil**

2 cups (2 lb/1 kg) shelled young, tender fava (broad) beans

3 cups (2 lb./1 kg) shelled peas

1 fennel bulb, trimmed, halved, and thinly sliced crosswise

³/₄ **lb. (375 g) asparagus, about 16 thin spears, tough ends removed, cut into 2-inch (5-cm) pieces**

2 red onions, halved and thinly sliced

1 tablespoon fresh lemon juice

2 teaspoons Dijon mustard

2 tablespoons finely chopped fresh dill

3 tablespoons extra-virgin olive oil

Preheat oven to 350ºF (180ºC/Gas 4). Season lamb with salt and pepper and drizzle with 2 tablespoons olive oil. Rub oil and seasonings into lamb, then place in roasting pan.

Place lamb in oven and roast until medium-rare and it springs back when pressed with fingertip, about 8 minutes. Remove lamb to carving board, cover loosely with aluminum foil, and let rest for 5 minutes before carving.

While lamb is roasting, bring large saucepan filled with salted water to boil over high heat. Add fava beans and peas and cook for 4 minutes. Add fennel and asparagus and continue to cook until beans and peas are tender and fennel and asparagus are tender-crisp, about 2 minutes longer. Drain vegetables and rinse under cold running water. Drain again and place in serving bowl.

In frying pan, heat remaining 2 tablespoons olive oil over high heat. Add onions and cook, stirring occasionally, until softened, about 4 minutes. Add to other vegetables.

In small bowl, whisk together lemon juice, mustard, and dill, then whisk in extra-virgin olive oil to make vinaigrette. Season with salt and pepper.

Cut lamb across grain into slices ¹/₄ inch (6 mm) thick and add to vegetables. Pour vinaigrette over salad and toss to combine. Serve immediately.

Serves 6

Lamb chops with mint pesto and mustard mashed potatoes

2 lb. (1 kg) red potatoes, about 7 medium, unpeeled

Mint pesto
3 cups (3 oz./90 g) fresh mint leaves
$1/3$ cup ($1^{1}/_{2}$ oz./45 g) pine nuts
$1/2$ cup (2 oz./60 g) grated Parmesan cheese
1 tablespoon fresh lemon juice
3 tablespoons olive oil

8 lamb loin chops from midloin, each about $1^{1}/_{2}$ inches (4 cm) thick
Salt and freshly ground black pepper
1 tablespoon olive oil
7 tablespoons ($3^{1}/_{2}$ oz./100 g) butter, at room temperature
1 tablespoon heavy (double) cream
2 tablespoons whole-grain mustard
2 cloves garlic, crushed

Preheat oven to 400°F (200°C/Gas 6).

In large saucepan, combine potatoes with salted water to cover by about 3 inches (7.5 cm). Place over high heat, bring to boil, and cook until tender when pierced with a knife, about 30 minutes.

While potatoes are cooking, make mint pesto: In food processor, combine mint, pine nuts, cheese, and lemon juice and process until roughly chopped. Add oil and puree until smooth. Transfer to covered container and refrigerate until needed.

Using dampened kitchen string, tie each lamb chop to hold tail in place. Place chops in roasting pan just large enough to accommodate them in single layer and season with salt and pepper. Drizzle oil evenly over chops.

Place lamb in oven and roast for 10 minutes. Reduce heat to 300°F (150°C/Gas 2) and continue roasting until thermometer inserted into thickest part away from bone registers 150°F (65°C) for medium, about 10 minutes longer. Remove lamb to warmed platter, cover loosely with aluminum foil, and let rest for 5 minutes.

When potatoes are ready, drain and, when just cool enough to handle, peel, place in bowl, and mash with potato masher until smooth. Alternatively, peel and pass through ricer held over bowl. Return potatoes to saucepan and add butter, cream, mustard, and garlic. Season with salt and pepper, place over medium heat, and stir until mixture is smooth and heated through.

Spoon bed of mashed potatoes on each warmed dinner plate, top with 2 lamb chops, and place a spoonful of mint pesto on the side.

Serves 4

Pork

Pork loin with sage and apples

1 boneless pork loin with rind intact,
  about 4$\frac{1}{2}$ lb. (2.25 kg), rolled and tied

1 tablespoon fennel seeds

2 tablespoons sea salt

2 teaspoons freshly ground black pepper

2 tablespoons olive oil

20 fresh sage leaves

8 small sweet baking apples, such as Gala or Pink
  Lady, with cores intact

Preheat oven to 400°F (200°C/Gas 6). Using sharp knife, score pork rind crosswise at $\frac{1}{4}$-inch (6-mm) intervals. Place pork in roasting pan. In mortar, roughly grind fennel seeds with pestle. Stir in salt and pepper. Sprinkle pork evenly with salt mixture, then rub mixture into scored rind. Drizzle pork evenly with oil. Push 5 sage leaves into each end of rolled pork. Arrange half of apples along each side of pork, then sprinkle apples evenly with remaining 10 sage leaves.

Place pork in oven and roast, basting apples occasionally with pan drippings, until rind is just starting to crackle, about 30 minutes. Reduce heat to 350°F (180°C/Gas 4) and continue roasting until rind is crisp and golden and thermometer inserted into thickest part of loin registers 155°F (70°C), or juices run clear when thin skewer is inserted into the center, about 1 hour and 10 minutes longer. Remove pork to carving board, cover loosely with aluminum foil, and let rest for 15 minutes before carving. Leave apples in pan in turned-off oven.

Snip strings and carve pork into slices $\frac{1}{4}$ inch (6 mm) thick. Arrange on warmed platter with apples.

Serves 8

Leg of pork with lime-and-mustard glaze

4 tablespoons lime marmalade

1 tablespoon grated lime zest

¼ cup (2 fl. oz./60 ml) fresh lime juice

1 cup (7 oz./220 g) firmly packed brown sugar

½ cup (4 oz./125 g) Dijon mustard

2 tablespoons olive oil

½ teaspoon ground cinnamon

¼ teaspoon ground cloves

Salt and freshly ground pepper

1 whole pork leg, about 10 lb. (5 kg), rind removed

Preheat oven to 325°F (170°C/Gas 3). Grease a large, flat rack at least 1 inch (2.5 cm) tall and place in roasting pan. Add water to pan to depth of 1 inch (2.5 cm).

In nonreactive bowl, combine lime marmalade and lime zest and juice and stir well. Add brown sugar, mustard, oil, cinnamon, and cloves and season with salt and pepper. Stir to combine. Place pork leg on prepared rack and season with salt and pepper. Pour half of lime mixture over leg, spreading to coat evenly.

Place leg in oven and roast, basting every 20 minutes with remaining lime mixture, until leg is evenly browned and thermometer inserted into thickest part away from bone registers 155°F (70°C), about 2½ hours. Remove leg to carving board, cover loosely with aluminum foil, and let rest for 15 minutes before carving.

Carve pork leg and arrange slices on warmed platter. Serve immediately.

Serves 12–15

Lemon-and-mint pork tenderloin with fig, feta, and hazelnut salad

½ cup (½ oz./15 g) fresh mint leaves

¼ cup (2 fl. oz./60 ml) fresh lemon juice

2 tablespoons olive oil

Salt and freshly ground black pepper

4 pork tenderloins (fillets), each about
 10 oz. (300 g) (see note)

Salad

⅓ cup (2 oz./60 g) hazelnuts (filberts)

6 fresh figs, stems trimmed, quartered lengthwise

⅔ cup (3½ oz./100 g) crumbled feta cheese

2 cups (2 oz./60 g) fresh mint leaves, roughly chopped

2 teaspoons fresh lemon juice

1 tablespoon olive oil

Salt and freshly ground black pepper

In mortar, roughly bruise mint leaves with pestle. Add lemon juice and olive oil, season with salt and pepper, and mix to combine. Place pork in shallow, nonreactive dish, pour in mint mixture, and turn pork to coat. Cover and refrigerate for at least 3 hours or up to 24 hours.

Position one oven rack in lower third of oven and another rack in upper third of oven and preheat to 400°F (200°C/Gas 6). Place a flat rack in roasting pan. Remove pork from marinade and pat thoroughly dry with paper towels. Place pork on rack and place in oven on upper rack. Roast until just firm to touch, about 17 minutes.

While pork is roasting, make salad: Spread hazelnuts on baking sheet, place on lower rack in oven, and toast until golden and aromatic, about 5 minutes. Remove and set aside for 5 minutes to cool slightly, then place in clean paper towel and rub vigorously between palms to remove skins. Roughly chop hazelnuts and place in bowl. Add figs, cheese, and mint. In small bowl, whisk together lemon juice and oil and season with salt and pepper. Pour over fig mixture and toss to combine.

When pork is ready, remove from oven and let rest for 5 minutes before serving.

Arrange pork tenderloins on dinner plates. Divide salad evenly among plates.

Serves 4

Note: If only larger pork tenderloins (fillets) can be found, buy enough to total about 2½ lb. (1.25 kg). They will roast in about the same amount of time. Thickly slice them and divide evenly among dinner plates.

Five-spice fresh bacon with roasted peach sauce

Serve with steamed baby bok choy.

**2¹/₃-lb. (1.3-kg) piece fresh bacon (pork belly) with
   rind intact**
2 tablespoons peanut oil
1 tablespoon sea salt
Freshly ground black pepper
1 tablespoon five-spice powder

Roasted peach sauce
**1¹/₄ lb. (625 g) freestone peaches, about 4, pitted and
   cut into wedges (see note)**
2 cinnamon sticks
4 star anise
1 tablespoon finely grated, peeled fresh ginger
1 tablespoon Chinese rice wine
2 teaspoons soy sauce
2 teaspoons cornstarch (cornflour)
¹/₂ cup (4 fl. oz./125 ml) chicken stock

Preheat oven to 425°F (220°C/Gas 7). Using sharp knife, score pork rind on diagonal at ¹/₄-inch (6-mm) intervals. Place pork in roasting pan. Drizzle oil over pork, sprinkle with salt, pepper, and five-spice powder, and rub oil and seasonings into rind.

Place pork in oven and roast until rind starts to crisp, about 30 minutes. Remove excess fat from pan, reduce heat to 325°F (170°C/Gas 3), and continue roasting until exterior has a nice crust and interior is tender throughout and almost falls apart when pressed firmly with a fork, about 2 hours longer. Remove pork to carving board, cover loosely with aluminum foil, and let rest for 15 minutes before carving. Raise oven heat to 350°F (180°C/Gas 4).

While pork is resting, make peach sauce: In roasting pan just large enough to accommodate peaches in single layer, combine peaches, cinnamon, and star anise. Place in oven and roast until peaches leach their juices, about 10 minutes. Remove from oven, discard cinnamon and star anise, and transfer peaches and juice to saucepan. Place over medium heat and add ginger, wine, and soy sauce. Stir to combine and bring to simmer. In small bowl, dissolve cornstarch in stock. Add to peaches and cook, stirring occasionally, until sauce thickens slightly, about 5 minutes.

Cut pork across grain into slices 1 inch (2.5 cm) thick. Serve immediately with warm peach sauce.

Serves 6

Note: If freestone peaches are unavailable, cling peaches may be substituted. Neither type needs to be peeled for making the sauce.

Chicken

Chicken with Asian spices

Serve with steamed jasmine rice (see note, page 37).

1 chicken, 3 lb. (1.5 kg)
3 tablespoons soy sauce
1 tablespoon peanut oil
2 teaspoons Asian sesame oil
2 tablespoons honey
6 star anise
3 cinnamon sticks
6 cardamom pods, bruised
3 cloves garlic, sliced
1 lime

Remove neck from chicken cavity and reserve. Rinse chicken inside and out with cold running water and pat thoroughly dry with paper towels. Tuck wing tips under and truss legs with dampened string. Place on shallow platter with neck.

In small bowl, combine soy sauce, oils, honey, star anise, cinnamon, cardamom, and garlic to make a marinade. Brush marinade over chicken. Cover and refrigerate for 1 hour.

Preheat oven to 400°F (200°C/Gas 6). Place flat rack in roasting pan. Stack 2 large sheets parchment (baking) paper on rack. Remove chicken from platter, reserving marinade, and place in center of paper. Slip neck alongside. Brush chicken with reserved marinade. Using vegetable peeler, remove lime zest in single long, narrow strip, allowing it to fall onto the breast of chicken. Bring paper up and over chicken and fold edges over to enclose bird completely. Secure closed with bamboo skewers that have been soaked in water for 30 minutes, or with staples.

Roast chicken until thermometer inserted in thickest part of thigh away from bone registers 175°F (80°C), 50–55 minutes. Alternatively, pierce thigh joint with thin skewer; chicken is ready when juices run clear. Remove chicken to carving board, cover loosely with parchment from pan, and let rest for at least 10 minutes before carving.

Carve chicken, arrange on platter, and serve hot or at room temperature.

Serves 4

Ricotta-stuffed chicken breasts with mushrooms and lentils

4 skin-on, boneless chicken breast halves, each about 7 oz. (220 g)
Ricotta Cheese Stuffing (page 25)

Lentils
1 tablespoon olive oil
1 yellow (brown) onion, roughly chopped
2 cloves garlic, thinly sliced
3 fresh thyme sprigs
7 oz. (220 g) speck (see note), cut into 1/3-inch (1-cm) pieces
1 2/3 cups (11 oz./330 g) Puy lentils (see note)
3 cups (24 fl. oz./750 ml) chicken stock
2 tablespoons butter, at room temperature

10 oz. (300 g) fresh white (cup) mushrooms, about 14, 2 inches (5 cm) in diameter, stem ends trimmed, quartered
3 1/2 oz. (100 g) fresh shiitake mushrooms, about 10, stems removed, quartered
5 oz. (150 g) fresh oyster mushrooms, about 14, stem ends trimmed, halved lengthwise
1/4 cup (2 fl. oz./60 ml) olive oil
Salt and freshly ground black pepper

Preheat oven to 350°F (180°C/Gas 4). Rinse chicken breasts with cold running water and pat thoroughly dry with paper towels. Using fingers, and working from pointed end of each breast, carefully loosen skin, being careful not to tear it and keeping it attached along other edges. Spoon stuffing between skin and flesh, dividing it evenly between breasts, and then secure skin on each breast with toothpick. Set aside.

To make lentils: In frying pan, heat oil over high heat. Add onion, garlic, and thyme and cook, stirring, until softened, about 5 minutes. Add speck and cook, stirring, until browned, about 2 minutes. Add lentils and stock, bring to boil, reduce heat to low, and simmer, uncovered, until stock is almost absorbed and lentils are tender, about 40 minutes.

While lentils are cooking, select roasting pan large enough to accommodate breasts in single layer. Place mushrooms in pan, drizzle with 2 tablespoons olive oil, season with salt and pepper, and toss to coat evenly. Place chicken breasts on top of mushrooms, drizzle evenly with remaining 2 tablespoons oil, and season with salt and pepper. Place pan in oven and roast until chicken skin is golden brown and mushrooms have softened, about 35 minutes.

When lentils are ready, stir in butter and season to taste with salt and pepper.

Spoon lentils on warmed dinner plates and top with chicken breasts. Serve mushrooms on the side.

Serves 4

Note: Speck, a brine-cured or smoked bacon, is a specialty of Alto-Aldige, in northeastern Italy. Bacon can be substituted.

Puy lentils are tiny, deep-green lentils that hold their shape nicely when cooked. They originated in the area around Le Puy, in central France, but are now grown elsewhere as well.

Whole chicken with lemon and thyme

1 lb. (500 g) turnips, about 3 medium, peeled and
    quartered

1½ lb. (750 g) sweet potatoes, about 1 small, peeled
    and cut into 2-inch (5-cm) pieces

10 oz. (300 g) carrots, about 3 medium, peeled and cut
    into 2-inch (5-cm) lengths

10 oz. (300 g) parsnips, about 1–2 medium, peeled and
    cut into 2-inch (5-cm) lengths

1 small butternut squash (pumpkin), 1 lb. (500 g),
    halved, seeded, peeled, and cut into 2-inch
    (5-cm) pieces

¼ cup (2 fl. oz./60 ml) olive oil

Salt and freshly ground black pepper

1 chicken, 3½ lb. (1.75 kg)

1 lemon, halved

1 head garlic, halved crosswise

1 bunch fresh thyme

2 lb. (1 kg) baking potatoes, about 7 medium, each
    about 4 inches (10 cm) long, peeled and halved
    crosswise

½ cup (4 fl. oz./125 ml) white wine

Position one oven rack in lower third of oven and another oven rack in upper third of oven and preheat to 375°F (190°C/Gas 5). In roasting pan large enough to hold vegetables in single layer, combine turnips, sweet potatoes, carrots, parsnips, and squash. Drizzle vegetables with 2 tablespoons olive oil, season with salt and pepper, toss to coat evenly, and spread in single layer. Place pan in oven on lower rack and roast for 15 minutes.

Meanwhile, remove neck from chicken cavity and reserve. Rinse chicken inside and out with cold running water and pat thoroughly dry with paper towels. Season chicken cavity with salt and pepper. Squeeze lemon halves over chicken and place rinds inside cavity with half each of garlic and thyme. Truss chicken (page 15), then place, breast side up, in separate roasting pan and add remaining garlic and chicken neck to pan. Season skin with salt and pepper and drizzle with 1 tablespoon oil. Rub salt, pepper, and oil evenly into skin. Add potatoes to pan, season them with salt and pepper, and drizzle with remaining 1 tablespoon oil.

Place chicken in oven on upper rack and roast chicken and vegetables, basting chicken every 15–20 minutes with remaining half bunch of thyme dipped in pan drippings, until skin and potatoes are golden brown and thermometer inserted into thickest part of thigh away from bone registers 175°F (80°C), about 1 hour and 10 minutes. Alternatively, pierce thigh joint with thin skewer; chicken is ready when juices run clear. Remove chicken to carving board, cover loosely with aluminum foil, and let rest 15 minutes before carving.

Reduce oven heat to 200°F (100°C/Gas ¼). Add potatoes to vegetables in second pan and return to oven to keep warm until serving time.

To make pan sauce: Pour contents of pan into clear glass measuring pitcher, let stand for a minute or so, and then spoon fat off surface. Return defatted drippings to pan. Alternatively, pour off fat from pan, leaving defatted juices in pan. Place pan on stove top over high heat. Bring to boil, add wine, and deglaze pan, using a wooden spoon to scrape up browned-on bits from pan bottom and pressing against garlic to free cloves from papery sheaths. Cook juices until reduced by half, about 2 minutes, then remove from heat.

Carve chicken and arrange on warmed platter. Pour pan sauce through a fine-mesh sieve, drizzling evenly over chicken. Serve with roasted vegetables.

Serves 4–6

Variations

For pan juices with more pronounced garlic flavor, add extra head of garlic, halved crosswise, to pan at start of roasting.

Use other citrus fruits, such as limes or oranges, in place of lemons.

Substitute 1 bunch fresh rosemary for thyme. Rub chicken with 1 tablespoon fennel seeds, roughly crushed, when rubbing with oil, salt, and pepper.

Poussins with mustard-and-quince stuffing

4 poussins (spatchcocks), about 1 lb. (500 g) each (see note)

8 bay leaves

2 cups (4 oz./125 g) fresh bread crumbs

2 teaspoons dry mustard (mustard powder)

½ cup (4 oz./125 g) quince paste, finely chopped (see note)

6 fresh sage leaves, roughly chopped

3 tablespoons olive oil

Salt and freshly ground black pepper

Preheat oven to 350°F (180°C/Gas 4). Rinse poussins inside and out with cold running water and pat thoroughly dry with paper towels. Tuck wing tips under. Using fingers and starting from body cavity, carefully loosen skin on breast of each poussin, being careful not to tear skin. Slip 2 bay leaves under skin of each poussin, positioning 1 leaf over each breast.

In bowl, combine bread crumbs, dry mustard, quince paste, sage leaves, and 2 tablespoons olive oil. Season with salt and pepper and mix well to make stuffing.

Spoon one-fourth of stuffing into body cavity of each poussin. (There is no need to truss legs.) Place poussins, breast side up, in roasting pan, season with salt and pepper, and drizzle evenly with remaining 1 tablespoon olive oil.

Place pan in oven and roast poussins until golden brown and a thermometer inserted into thickest part of thigh away from bone registers 175°F (80°C), 35–40 minutes. Alternatively, pierce thigh joint of poussin with thin skewer; poussin is ready when juices run clear.

To serve, arrange poussins on warmed platter. Pour off fat from pan drippings, then drizzle defatted juices over poussins.

Serves 4

Note: Poussins are young chickens, usually weighing 1 lb. (500 g) or less. Cornish hens can be substituted. Quince paste, made by cooking quince pulp with a large measure of sugar, is commonly eaten with a white, mild cheese for dessert in Latin America, Spain, and Portugal. Look for it in markets that carry Iberian or Latin American foods.

Chicken legs with spiced butter and couscous

6 whole chicken legs (Marylands), about 11 oz. (330 g)
  each
$\frac{1}{2}$ cup (4 oz./125 g) butter, at room temperature
1 teaspoon ground coriander
1 teaspoon ground cumin
$\frac{1}{2}$ teaspoon ground paprika
$\frac{1}{4}$ teaspoon ground allspice
$\frac{1}{2}$ teaspoon ground ginger
$\frac{1}{2}$ teaspoon ground cinnamon
Sea salt and freshly ground black pepper
2 tablespoons olive oil

Couscous

1 small butternut squash (pumpkin), 1$\frac{1}{2}$ lb.
  (750 g), halved, peeled, seeded, and cut
  into $\frac{1}{3}$-inch (1-cm) pieces
$\frac{1}{4}$ cup (2 fl. oz./60 ml) olive oil
Salt and freshly ground black pepper
2 yellow (brown) onions, halved and thinly sliced
2 cups (10 oz./300 g) instant couscous
$\frac{1}{3}$ cup (2 oz./60 g) golden raisins (sultanas)
1$\frac{1}{2}$ cups (12 fl. oz./375 ml) boiling water
2 tablespoons butter, at room temperature, roughly
  chopped
1 cup (1 oz./30 g) fresh cilantro (fresh coriander) leaves

Position one oven rack in lower third of oven and second oven rack in upper third of oven and preheat to 350°F (180°C/Gas 4).

A small portion of backbone is usually attached to thigh bone on whole legs. Using small, sharp knife, cut through thigh joint and remove backbone portion. Rinse legs with cold running water and pat thoroughly dry with paper towels. In small bowl, combine butter and ground spices and season with salt and pepper. Using fork, mix together until well combined. Using fingers, carefully loosen skin on top of each chicken leg. Spoon about one-sixth of butter mixture between skin and flesh on each chicken leg, distributing it evenly.

Place chicken legs in roasting pan, drizzle evenly with 2 tablespoons olive oil, and season with salt and pepper. Place pan in oven on lower rack and roast until skin is golden brown and juices run clear when thigh joint is pierced with thin skewer, about 40 minutes.

Meanwhile, make couscous: Spread squash pieces in single layer on rimmed baking sheet. Drizzle with 2 tablespoons oil, season with salt and pepper, toss to coat evenly, and again spread out in single layer. Place on upper rack and roast until golden brown and tender, about 30 minutes.

In frying pan, heat remaining 2 tablespoons oil over medium heat. Add onions and cook, stirring occasionally, until dark brown and crispy, 10–15 minutes. Set aside.

In heatproof bowl, combine couscous and raisins. Pour in boiling water, stir to combine, and cover with plastic wrap. Set aside until water has been absorbed, about 5 minutes. Fluff couscous with fork, add butter, and stir gently until butter melts. Add squash pieces, onions, and cilantro, season with salt and pepper, and stir gently to combine.

Spoon couscous onto warmed dinner plates, dividing evenly, and top with chicken legs. Spoon pan juices over chicken and serve.

Serves 6

Turkey

Stuffed whole turkey with cranberry sauce

1 turkey, about 8 lb. (4 kg)
Bread and Herb Stuffing (page 24)
4 tablespoons butter, at room temperature
Salt and freshly ground black pepper
Cranberry Sauce (page 27)

Preheat oven to 350°F (180°C/Gas 4). Rinse turkey inside and outside with cold running water and pat thoroughly dry with paper towels. Tuck wing tips under, then spoon stuffing into body cavity and truss legs together with kitchen string. Place turkey in roasting pan and rub turkey with 3½ tablespoons butter. Brush remaining ½ tablespoon butter on piece of aluminum foil large enough to cover breast. Season turkey with salt and pepper and place foil over turkey breast.

Place turkey in oven and roast for 2 hours, removing foil every 20 minutes and basting bird with pan drippings. Remove foil from turkey, raise heat to 425°F (220°C/Gas 7), and continue roasting until turkey is golden and thermometer inserted in thickest part of thigh away from bone registers 175°F (80°C), about 20 minutes longer. Remove turkey to carving board, cover loosely with aluminum foil, and let rest for 10 minutes before carving.

Snip string and spoon stuffing into warmed serving bowl. Carve turkey as directed on page 16 and arrange on warmed platter. Serve with cranberry sauce.

Serves 10

Middle Eastern couscous-stuffed turkey breast

1 whole turkey breast (buffe), about 8 lb. (4 kg)
Couscous Stuffing (page 24)
¼ cup (2 fl. oz./60 ml) olive oil
Salt and freshly ground black pepper
Middle Eastern Rub (page 22)

Preheat oven to 350°F (180°C/Gas 4). Rinse turkey breast with cold running water and pat thoroughly dry with paper towels. Place on cutting board. Using sharp knife, cut along each side of breastbone. Continue to cut, following rib cage on each side and cutting through joints that connect wings, to divide breast in half and free both halves of all bones. Place one breast half on board, and starting at long side, butterfly it by cutting horizontally through thickest part, stopping within about 1 inch (2.5 cm) of opposite side. Repeat with second breast. Open out one breast, cut side up, on board. Cover with parchment (baking) paper and, using meat mallet, flatten evenly to about 1 inch (2.5 cm) thickness. Repeat with remaining breast.

Divide stuffing evenly between breasts, placing it in line down center along length. Starting from long side on one breast, fold over end, fold in sides, and then roll up into cylinder. Tie at 3-inch (7.5-cm) intervals with dampened kitchen string. Repeat with remaining breast. Brush breasts with oil, season with salt and pepper, and sprinkle evenly with Middle Eastern rub. Wrap each breast in aluminum foil and place in roasting pan.

Place turkey in oven and roast for 1 hour. Remove foil and continue roasting until turkey is golden brown and springs back when pressed with fingertip, about 30 minutes longer. Remove turkey rolls to carving board, cover loosely with aluminum foil, and let rest for 10 minutes before carving.

Snip strings and carve turkey rolls into thick slices. Serve immediately.

Serves 10

Sherry-marinated turkey legs with piri piri sauce

2 whole turkey legs (Marylands), each about
1¹/₃ lb. (650 g)
Salt and freshly ground black pepper
1 tablespoon sweet paprika
1 yellow (brown) onion, halved and thinly sliced
2 carrots, peeled and roughly chopped
6 juniper berries
¹/₄ cup (2 fl. oz./60ml) olive oil
2¹/₂ cups (20 fl. oz./625 ml) dry sherry
Piri Piri Sauce (page 26)

Rinse turkey legs with cold running water and pat thoroughly dry with paper towels. Place legs in nonreactive dish. Season with salt and pepper and sprinkle with paprika, then rub seasonings into skin. Add onion, carrots, and juniper berries, and drizzle legs and vegetables with 2 tablespoons oil. Pour sherry into dish and stir to mix well. Cover and refrigerate for at least 3 hours or up to 3 days.

Preheat oven to 350°F (180°C/Gas 4). Remove turkey from marinade and pat thoroughly dry with paper towels. Place turkey legs in roasting pan just large enough to accommodate them and drizzle with remaining 2 tablespoons oil. Place turkey in oven and roast until golden brown and juices run clear when thin skewer is inserted into thigh joint, about 40 minutes. Remove turkey legs to carving board, cover loosely with aluminum foil, and let rest for 10 minutes before carving.

Slice meat from turkey legs and arrange on warmed platter. Serve with piri piri sauce.

Serves 4

Duck

Whole duck with orange and sage

1 duck, about 4¼ lb (2.1 kg)

Sea salt and freshly ground black pepper

1 orange, quartered

¼ cup (¼ oz./7 g) fresh sage leaves

2 tablespoons olive oil

½ cup (4 oz./125 g) Candied Kumquats (page 29)

Preheat oven to 350°F (180°C/Gas 4). Place V-shaped or flat rack in roasting pan. Rinse duck inside and out with cold running water and pat thoroughly dry with paper towels. Using thin skewer, prick duck breasts all over, piercing skin. Season skin and cavity with salt and pepper, then place orange quarters and sage in cavity. Place duck on rack and drizzle with oil.

Place duck in oven and roast for 1 hour. Reduce heat to 300°F (150°C/Gas 2) and continue roasting until skin is crisp and golden and flesh is tender when pierced with knife, about 1½ hours longer.

Remove duck to carving board. Cut duck into portions on bone, or carve duck meat from body. Serve with candied kumquats.

Serves 2

Duck legs with ginger and soba noodles

4 whole duck legs, about ¹/₂ lb. (250 g) each

¹/₂ cup (¹/₄ lb./125 g) fresh ginger, peeled and finely grated

7 tablespoons (3¹/₂ fl. oz./100 ml) mirin (see note)

¹/₄ cup (2 fl. oz./60 ml) rice vinegar

2 teaspoons soy sauce

3 English (hothouse) or Lebanese cucumbers, thinly sliced crosswise

1 teaspoon salt, plus extra for cooking noodles

3 oz. (90 g) dried soba noodles (see note)

2 tablespoons sliced pink pickled ginger (see note)

2 tablespoons finely chopped fresh chives

Preheat oven to 350°F (180°C/Gas 4). Place duck legs in roasting pan just large enough to accommodate them and sprinkle evenly with fresh ginger, mirin, vinegar, and soy sauce. Cover with aluminum foil, place in oven, and roast for 45 minutes. Remove foil and continue roasting until skin is crisp and dark brown, about 20 minutes longer.

While duck is roasting, combine cucumbers and 1 teaspoon salt in bowl, mix well, cover, and set aside for 30 minutes. Bring large saucepan filled with salted water to boil over high heat, add noodles, and cook until just tender, about 4 minutes. Drain noodles in colander and rinse well under cold running water. Set aside.

Gently squeeze excess water from cucumbers and place in clean bowl. Add pickled ginger and mix until well combined.

Remove duck legs from oven and divide among warmed dinner plates. Sprinkle chives evenly over duck legs. Place one-fourth each of noodles and cucumbers alongside each duck leg and serve immediately.

Serves 4

Note: Mirin is a sweetened rice wine used only for cooking. Soba noodles, available dried and fresh, are made from a mixture of buckwheat and wheat flour. Pink pickled ginger, known as gari *and commonly served alongside sushi and sashimi, is sold sliced in plastic tubs. Look for all three items in Japanese markets or well-stocked grocery stores.*

Fish and shellfish

Whole salmon with fennel and herbs

1 fennel bulb
2 teaspoons fennel seeds
1 cup (1 oz./30 g) fresh basil leaves
8 fresh thyme sprigs
1 red onion, halved and thinly sliced crosswise
Grated zest of 1 lemon
Sea salt and freshly ground black pepper
¼ cup (2 fl. oz./60 ml) olive oil
1 whole salmon, 4½ lb. (2.25 kg), cleaned

Preheat oven to 350°F (180°C/Gas 4). Using sharp knife, trim fennel bulb, then halve lengthwise, trim away tough core portion, and thinly slice crosswise. Place fennel in large bowl, add fennel seeds, basil, thyme, onion, and lemon zest, and season with salt and pepper. Drizzle with 2 tablespoons oil and toss to combine.

Rinse inside and outside of salmon with cold running water and pat thoroughly dry with paper towels. Season cavity with salt and pepper. Place salmon in roasting pan and spoon fennel mixture into cavity. Drizzle salmon with remaining 2 tablespoons olive oil and season with salt and pepper.

Place salmon in oven and roast until flesh is opaque throughout and flakes when tested with knife tip, about 45 minutes. Remove salmon from oven and serve immediately with stuffing.

Serves 6

Scallops with grapefruit and coriander seeds

Approx. 3¹/₂ cups (2 lb./1 kg) rock salt

12 scallops on half shell (see note)

1 tablespoon coriander seeds

Sea salt and freshly ground black pepper

2 tablespoons extra-virgin olive oil

¹/₄ cup (2 fl. oz./60 ml) fresh grapefruit juice

¹/₃ cup (¹/₃ oz./10 g) fresh cilantro (fresh coriander)
   leaves

Preheat oven to 425°F (220°C/Gas 7). Pour rock salt evenly over base of roasting pan. It should be ¹/₂ inch (12 mm) deep. Arrange scallops in pan, pressing them into rock salt so they remain level.

In small frying pan, toast coriander seeds over medium heat, stirring occasionally, until fragrant, about 4 minutes. Remove from heat and set aside for 5 minutes to cool slightly. In mortar, roughly crush coriander seeds with pestle.

Season scallops with salt, pepper, and crushed coriander, and drizzle with oil. Place scallops in oven and roast until plump and opaque throughout, about 5 minutes. Pour 1 teaspoon grapefruit juice over each scallop, top with cilantro leaves, and serve immediately.

Serves 6

Note: If scallops on the half shell are unavailable, purchase 12 natural scallop shells at a cookware store. Place 12 shucked scallops in them and nest in rock salt.

Whole snapper in salt crust with tamarind-chili sauce

11 cups (6 lb./3 kg) rock salt
2 whole red snappers, each 3 lb. (1.5 kg), cleaned
3 limes, quartered

Tamarind-chili sauce
$^1/_2$ cup (5 oz./150 g) tamarind pulp (see note)
$^1/_2$ cup (4 fl. oz./125 ml) boiling water
2 tablespoons sugar
1 teaspoon fish sauce (see note, page 22)

1 cup (1 oz./30 g) fresh cilantro (fresh coriander) leaves
1 cup (1 oz./30 g) fresh mint leaves
1 long, red fresh chili pepper
$^1/_4$ cup (1 oz./30 g) fried onions (see note)

Preheat oven to 350°F (180°C/Gas 4). Spread half of rock salt in roasting pan; it should be 3–4 inches (7.5–10 cm) deep. Rinse inside and outside of fish with cold running water and pat thoroughly dry with paper towels. Place fish on bed of salt. Divide lime quarters evenly between fish cavities. Cover fish with remaining rock salt.

Place fish in oven and roast until flesh is opaque throughout and flakes when tested with knife tip (you will need to scrape away salt near center of fish to test), about 50 minutes.

While fish are roasting, make tamarind-chili sauce: In small, heatproof bowl, cover tamarind pulp with boiling water and let stand for 4 minutes. Pour through sieve, pressing solids with back of spoon to extract as much flavor as possible. Discard solids. Add sugar and fish sauce to tamarind juice and stir to combine.

Just before fish are done, in large bowl (large size avoids bruising herb leaves), combine cilantro, mint, chili, and onions and stir to mix.

Remove fish from oven, scrape away top salt layer, and transfer fish to warmed serving platter. Peel away skin from top of each fish. Drizzle half of tamarind-chili sauce over top fillets, sprinkle with half of herb mixture, and serve. When top fillets have been removed, remove backbone and lift away bottom fillets from skin. Drizzle bottom fillets with remaining sauce, sprinkle with remaining herb mixture, and serve.

Serves 6

Note: Reddish-brown tamarind pulp comes from the pods of a tropical tree. It is sold in blocks wrapped in plastic in Asian markets. Fried onions, commonly used to garnish Asian dishes, are thinly sliced yellow (brown) onions that are deep-fried until browned and crisp. They are sold in Asian markets. If unavailable, look for fried onions, used for salads, in supermarkets.

Salmon steaks with bay and chervil

Serve on a bed of young leeks (see note).

6 salmon steaks (cutlets), about 6 oz. (180 g) each
4 cloves garlic, thinly sliced
12 fresh bay leaves
1/2 cup (1/2 oz./15 g) fresh chervil leaves
Sea salt and freshly ground black pepper
1 tablespoon olive oil
Juice of 2 limes or lemons
Extra olive oil for serving (optional)

Preheat oven to 350°F (180°C/Gas 4). Place salmon steaks in roasting pan just large enough to accommodate them. Sprinkle each steak with equal amount of garlic, bay leaves, and chervil leaves. Season with salt and pepper and drizzle evenly with oil and citrus juice.

Place fish in oven and roast until flesh is opaque throughout and flakes when tested with knife tip, about 15 minutes. Remove from oven and serve immediately on warmed dinner plates. Drizzle with extra olive oil, if desired.

Serves 6

Note: Leeks can be steamed or braised in chicken stock over medium heat for 8–10 minutes.

Tuna on red bell peppers, olives, and anchovies

Serve with green salad.

3-lb. (1.5-kg) piece yellowfin tuna fillet, skin removed

12 anchovy fillets packed in olive oil

¼ cup (2 fl. oz./60 ml) olive oil

3 red bell peppers (capsicums), seeded and thinly sliced

**1 yellow (brown) onion, halved and thinly sliced
  crosswise**

3 cloves garlic, thinly sliced

½ cup (½ oz./15 g) fresh marjoram leaves

½ cup (2½ oz./75 g) niçoise olives

1 tablespoon red-wine vinegar

2 teaspoons white sugar

Sea salt and freshly ground black pepper

Preheat oven to 350°F (180°C/Gas 4). Using small, sharp knife, make 6 equally spaced slits, each about ½ inch (12 mm) deep, in tuna, and stuff 1 anchovy fillet in each slit. Place tuna in roasting pan.

Place tuna in oven and roast until flesh is opaque throughout and flakes when tested with knife tip, about 40 minutes.

While tuna is roasting, in a small Dutch oven (heavy-based casserole dish), heat oil over medium heat on stove top. Add bell peppers, onion, and garlic, and cook, stirring occasionally, until softened, about 10 minutes. Add marjoram, olives, vinegar, sugar, salt, pepper, and remaining 6 anchovy fillets. Continue to cook, stirring occasionally, until flavors are blended, about 2 minutes longer. Cover and remove from heat.

Remove tuna to carving board and cut across grain into thick slices. Divide slices evenly among warmed dinner plates and serve warm braised bell peppers alongside.

Serves 6

Vegetables

Slow-roasted eggplant with tomato and garlic

2 eggplants (aubergines), about
   1¼ lb. (625 g) each
2 cans (13 oz./400 g each) whole tomatoes
   with juices
Pinch superfine (caster) sugar
Salt and freshly ground black pepper
4 cloves garlic, thinly sliced
¾ cup (6 fl. oz./180 ml) olive oil

Preheat oven to 350°F (180°C/Gas 4). Using sharp knife, trim off stem and blossom ends from each eggplant, then cut crosswise into slices ¼ inch (6 mm) thick.

In blender, place tomatoes and pulse until smooth. Season tomato with sugar to balance acidity and then with salt and pepper.

In shallow two-quart (two-liter) baking dish, arrange layer of eggplant slices, overlapping them slightly. Sprinkle some garlic slices over top, season with salt and pepper, and drizzle evenly with 2 tablespoons olive oil. Spoon some tomato puree over eggplant. Continue layering until all eggplant has been used, ending with tomato puree. You should have 6 layers. Cover baking dish with aluminum foil.

Place eggplant in oven and roast until soft when tested with knife tip, about 1½ hours. Remove foil and continue roasting until tomato has reduced to thick sauce consistency, about 30 minutes longer. Remove from oven, set aside for 10 minutes to settle, then cut into squares and serve.

Serves 6

Mixed spring vegetables

2 red onions, each cut into 6 wedges
6 cloves garlic, peeled but left whole
4 small zucchini (courgettes), about 1 lb. (500 g) total weight, trimmed and cut in half lengthwise
3 baby fennel bulbs, trimmed and cut in half lengthwise or 1 large fennel bulb, cut lengthwise into slices 1/2 inch (12 mm) thick
1/4 cup (2 fl. oz./60 ml) olive oil
Salt and freshly ground black pepper
3/4 lb. (375 g) green asparagus, about 16 thin spears, trimmed
3/4 lb. (375 g) purple asparagus, about 8 thin spears, trimmed (see note)

Preheat oven to 350°F (180°C/Gas 4). On rimmed baking sheet large enough to hold all vegetables in single layer, combine onions, garlic, zucchini, and fennel. Drizzle with oil, season with salt and pepper, toss to combine, and again spread out in single layer.

Place vegetables in oven and roast for 20 minutes. Add asparagus to baking sheet, return to oven, and continue roasting until all vegetables are golden brown and tender when pierced with knife tip, about 20 minutes longer. Serve immediately.

Serves 6

Note: If you cannot find purple asparagus, use 1 1/2 lb. (750 g) green asparagus.

Mixed autumn vegetables

1 piece kabocha squash (pumpkin), 1-lb. (500-g), seeded (see note)
3/4 lb. (375 g) sweet potatoes, about 1 medium, peeled and cut into 3/4-inch (2-cm) pieces
12 baby turnips, tops trimmed and peeled
12 baby beets (beetroots), tops trimmed
14 oz. (440 g) parsnips, about 2 medium, peeled and quartered lengthwise
10 oz. (300 g) shallots (French shallots), about 6, peeled and left whole
1/4 cup (2 fl. oz./60 ml) olive oil
Salt and freshly ground black pepper

Preheat oven to 350°F (180°C/Gas 4). Using sharp knife, cut squash into crescents 3/4 inch (2 cm) thick. In roasting pan large enough to hold all vegetables in single layer, combine squash, sweet potatoes, turnips, beets, parsnips, and shallots. Drizzle with oil, season with salt and pepper, toss to combine, and again spread out in single layer.

Place vegetables in oven and roast until golden brown and tender when pierced with knife tip, about 1 hour. Remove from oven and keep vegetables hot, but let beets cool enough to be handled, then peel off skins. Return beets to other vegetables and serve immediately.

Serves 6

Note: Kabocha squash, also known as Japanese squash, looks like a small pumpkin, but has green speckled skin that roasts up sweet and soft enough to eat along with the yellow-orange flesh.

Paprika potatoes

1 cup (5 oz./150 g) all-purpose (plain) flour
1 teaspoon sweet paprika
3 lb. (1.5 kg) baking potatoes, about 10, not more than
   4 inches (10 cm) long, peeled and halved crosswise
3 tablespoons rendered goose fat or olive oil
Salt and freshly ground black pepper

Preheat oven to 350°F (180°C/Gas 4). In large bowl, stir
together flour and paprika. Working in batches, add potatoes
and toss to coat evenly, then shake off excess flour.

   Put goose fat or oil in roasting pan and place in oven until
hot, about 5 minutes. Add potatoes to pan, spreading in
single layer, and season with salt and pepper. Roast, turning
occasionally, until crisp and golden brown and tender when
pierced with knife tip, about 1 hour and 10 minutes. Serve
immediately.

Serves 6

Potatoes with rosemary and olive oil

2 lb. (1 kg) small potatoes (chats), about 18, preferably
   new potatoes, 1–2 inches (2.5–5 cm) in diameter
2 tablespoons olive oil
2 teaspoons sea salt
Freshly ground black pepper
Leaves from 2 rosemary sprigs

Preheat oven to 375°F (190°C/Gas 5). Place potatoes in
single layer in roasting pan. Drizzle with oil, sprinkle with salt,
pepper, and rosemary, toss to combine, and again spread
out in single layer.

   Place potatoes in oven and roast until golden brown and
tender when pierced with knife tip, about 40 minutes. Serve
immediately.

Serves 4–6

Potato stacks
(potatoes Anna)

3½ lb. (1.75 kg) waxy, oval, yellow-fleshed potatoes,
   about 24 medium
4 tablespoons butter, melted
Sea salt and freshly ground black pepper
2 tablespoons olive oil

Preheat oven to 400°F (200°C/Gas 6). Line two rimmed baking sheets with parchment (baking) paper. Fill large bowl with cold water. Peel and thinly slice potatoes crosswise, immediately adding slices to water. When all are sliced, drain and dry potatoes thoroughly with paper towels. Rinse and dry bowl and return sliced potatoes to it. Drizzle with butter, season with salt and pepper, and toss to combine.

Divide potato slices into 10 equal portions. Form each portion into round stack 4 inches (10 cm) in diameter on prepared baking sheets. Drizzle stacks evenly with oil.

Roast potatoes in oven until golden brown and tender when pierced with knife tip, about 40 minutes. Serve immediately.

Serves 10

Radicchio and Belgian endive wrapped in prosciutto

4 heads radicchio, halved lengthwise (see note)

4 heads Belgian endive (chicory/witloof), halved lengthwise

16 thin slices prosciutto

2 tablespoons olive oil

Salt and freshly ground black pepper

1 tablespoon balsamic vinegar

Preheat oven to 350°F (180°C/Gas 4). Wrap each radicchio half and Belgian endive half with prosciutto slice and secure with toothpick. Place in roasting pan in single layer. Drizzle evenly with olive oil and season with salt and pepper.

Place pan in oven and roast until Belgian endive is soft when tested with knife tip and prosciutto is crispy, about 30 minutes.

Remove from oven, drizzle radicchio and Belgian endive halves with balsamic vinegar, and serve immediately.

Serves 4

Note: You can use either round Verona radicchio or elongated Treviso radicchio for this recipe.

Fruit desserts

Apples stuffed with figs and walnuts

¼ cup (2 fl. oz./60 ml) brandy
¾ cup (5 oz./150 g) dried figs, roughly chopped
4 tablespoons unsalted butter, at room temperature,
  cut into small pieces
¼ cup (2 oz./60 g) packed brown sugar
½ cup (2 oz./60 g) walnuts, roughly chopped
1 teaspoon ground cinnamon
6 green apples, cored
Crème Anglaise (page 28)

Preheat oven to 350ºF (180ºC/Gas 4). In small saucepan, heat brandy over low heat. Place figs in small bowl, pour in warm brandy, and set aside to plump for 10 minutes.

Add butter, brown sugar, walnuts, and cinnamon to figs and mix until combined.

Spoon equal amount of fig mixture into center of each apple. Stand apples upright in roasting pan.

Place apples in oven and roast until tender when pierced with knife tip, about 30 minutes. Remove from oven and serve warm or at room temperature with crème anglaise.

Serves 6

Peaches and nectarines with amaretti topping

6 yellow-fleshed peaches, halved and pitted

6 white-fleshed nectarines, halved and pitted

5 oz. (150 g) roughly crushed amaretti, about 1¹/₂ cups

4 tablespoons butter, at room temperature, cut into
   ¹/₂-inch (12-mm) pieces

2 tablespoons superfine (caster) sugar

2 tablespoons all-purpose (plain) flour

Preheat oven to 350°F (180°C/Gas 4). Place peaches and nectarines, cut side up, in single layer in roasting pan. In bowl, combine amaretti, butter, sugar, and flour. Using fingers, mix together until just combined. Sprinkle mixture evenly over cut surface of peaches and nectarines.

Place pan in oven and roast until fruit is tender when pierced with knife tip and topping is golden brown, about 15 minutes. Remove from oven and serve hot or at room temperature.

Serves 4

Rhubarb and strawberries with rose water

1½ lb. (750 g) rhubarb, about 14, trimmed and cut
    into 2-inch (5-cm) lengths
⅓ cup (3 oz./90 g) superfine (caster) sugar
2 teaspoons rose water
½ teaspoon vanilla extract (essence)
1½ cups (½ lb./250 g) strawberries, hulled and halved
Vanilla ice cream for serving

Preheat oven to 350°F (180°C/Gas 4). Arrange rhubarb in single layer in baking dish. Sprinkle with sugar, drizzle with rose water and vanilla, toss to combine, and spread out in single layer again.

Place rhubarb in oven and roast until tender when pierced with knife tip, about 20 minutes. Add strawberries to dish and continue to roast until strawberries have softened, about 5 minutes longer.

Rhubarb and strawberries can be served warm or at room temperature. Divide them evenly among shallow dessert bowls. Add scoop of ice cream to each bowl. Drizzle juices from baking dish over fruit and ice cream and serve.

Serves 4

Honeyed figs with pistachio phyllo pastries

3 tablespoons unsalted butter
4 tablespoons honey
4 sheets phyllo pastry
½ cup (2 oz./60 g) pistachio nuts, roughly chopped
12 fresh figs, stems trimmed, halved lengthwise

Position one oven rack in lower third of oven and another oven rack in upper third of oven and preheat to 350°F (180°C/Gas 4).

In small saucepan, combine butter and 3 tablespoons honey. Place over medium heat and heat, stirring occasionally, until butter melts and mixture is smooth and fluid. Remove from heat and set aside to cool completely.

Line two rimmed baking sheets with parchment (baking) paper. Lay 1 phyllo sheet on clean cutting board. Keep remaining sheets covered with lightly dampened clean paper towel to prevent drying out. Brush phyllo sheet with butter-honey mixture, then sprinkle evenly with one-fourth of pistachios. Top with second phyllo sheet, brush with more butter-honey mixture, and sprinkle with one-third of remaining pistachios. Repeat with remaining 2 phyllo sheets, butter-honey mixture, and pistachios, stacking them on top of first 2 sheets. Using sharp knife, cut pastry stack in half lengthwise, and then in half crosswise, to create 4 rectangles. Cut each rectangle in half diagonally to create 2 triangles. Place 4 triangles on each prepared baking sheet.

Place 1 baking sheet on each oven rack and bake until pastry is golden brown, about 5 minutes. Remove from oven and let cool completely. Leave oven set at 350°F (180°C/Gas 4).

When pastries are almost cool, place figs, cut side up, on rimmed baking sheet. Drizzle evenly with remaining 1 tablespoon honey. Place figs on lower rack in oven and roast until soft when pierced with knife tip, about 10 minutes. Remove from oven.

Divide cooled pastry triangles among dessert plates, arrange warm roasted figs alongside, and serve.

Serves 4

Mixed berries on toasted brioche

1½ cups (8½ oz./250 g) strawberries, hulled and halved

1 cup (5 oz./150 g) blackberries

1 cup (5 oz./150 g) blueberries

1¾ cups (8 oz./250 g) raspberries

2 tablespoons superfine (caster) sugar

4 slices brioche, toasted and kept warm

1 cup (8 fl. oz./250 ml) heavy (double) cream

Preheat oven to 350°F (180°C/Gas 4). In large baking dish, combine all berries and sprinkle with sugar. Place berries in oven and roast until softened, about 10 minutes.

Place 1 warm slice brioche on each dessert plate. Spoon berries on top of brioche slices, dividing evenly. Top each with one-fourth of cream and serve immediately.

Serves 4

Glossary

Allspice A dried, cured, unripe berry from a tropical evergreen tree. Ground, it releases aromas of cloves, cinnamon, and nutmeg. Also known as "pimiento."

Amaretti Almond-flavored Italian cookies, which can be either crisp or soft.

Asian sesame oil Concentrated, intensely flavored oil extracted from the sesame seed should be used sparingly.

Balsamic vinegar A dark-colored, fragrant, sweet-tasting vinegar made from grapes. A wide range, of varying quality, is available.

Black mustard seeds Tiny, round, near-black seeds. Commonly used in curry powders and in many Indian vegetarian dishes and are carried in well-stocked grocery stores and Indian markets.

Cardamom Versatile spice used in both sweet and savory foods. A papery green pod containing black seeds with a slight camphor smell. When buying, select the greenest pods.

Chinese rice wine Made from glutinous rice, yeast, and spring water, and used in Chinese cooking, marinades, and sauces. Buy from Asian markets and grocery stores.

Cilantro (fresh coriander) The fresh leaf, stem, and root of the coriander plant. Not to be confused with coriander seed or ground coriander. Also known as "Chinese parsley."

Cinnamon The aromatic bark of a tropical tree, available ground or as rolled sticks or quills.

Couscous From the Middle East, these are flour-coated semolina pellets, similar to pasta. The instant variety takes 5 minutes to prepare, with the traditional taking at least an hour.

Cranberries, dried The dried form of the large red cranberry, most commonly known in America and Europe. With their sharp flavor, cranberries are commonly made into sauces and jellies to accompany poultry and game.

Fennel bulbs The aromatic, fleshy bulb of the fennel plant. Can be used raw in salads and the feathery fronds are used as a herb. Has an aniseed flavor but should not be confused with anise. The seeds are used as a spice in both Mediterranean and Indian cooking.

Fenugreek seeds Small, oblong, yellowish-brown seeds. Used in curry powders and in many Indian vegetarian dishes; carried in well-stocked grocery stores and Indian markets.

Figs Soft, raindrop-shaped fruit with green, brown, or purple skin. The inside is often bright pink with hundreds of tiny seeds. Its sweet honey taste has made it popular for thousands of years around the Mediterranean.

Five-spice powder A combination of ground star anise with fennel seeds, cassia or cinnamon, cloves, and black pepper.

Flageolet beans A light, green-tinged bean, traditionally eaten with lamb in France. Avaliable fresh, dried, or canned.

Flat-leaf (Italian) parsley With leaves similar to the tops of celery, this parsley variety has flat leaves. Used extensively in Italian and French cooking.

Ginger A tuberous rhizome native to southeast Asia and used extensively in the cuisine of this region. Its unique combination of hot, clean, and cool flavors are also used to aid digestion.

Horseradish A root that is used freshly grated or more

commonly in jar form. Has a sharp, hot, piquant flavor and can be used to accompany roast beef, fish, or chicken.

Juniper berries Dried blue-black berry with a pinelike smell. Used to flavor gin, it is often used to temper the rich flavors of game or fatty dishes.

Marjoram Closely related to oregano, this herb is smaller and softer with a less robust, sweeter flavor. Because of this quality, it is used where the flavor should not be too dominant.

Oyster mushrooms A delicately flavored mushroom, usually pale gray-brown in color. Available fresh from good markets and well-stocked grocery stores.

Pancetta Italian-style salted pork belly with a rich, baconlike flavor. Available from good delicatessens and well-stocked supermarkets.

Phyllo pastry A light, tissue-thin pastry that is layered with some type of fat, generally butter, to produce a crunchy, flaky result when baked.

Pine nuts Found inside pinecones, they have a sweet flavor and soft texture. They add a crunchy texture to pastas and salads and are used in pesto sauce.

Pistachio nuts Native to Syria, this small green nut is encased in a cream-colored shell, with a natural opening on one side.

Prosciutto Italian-style, slightly salted, air-dried ham commonly used in paper-thin slices. Available from good delicatessens and well-stocked supermarkets.

Shiitake mushrooms Asian mushrooms with a strong flavor and texture that hold their shape well when cooked.

Star anise A fragrant, star-shaped dried fruit containing small brown seeds. Commonly used whole.

Vanilla bean The cured seed pod of a tropical climbing orchid. Used to flavor sweet foods such as ice cream, cake, and custard. Look for dark brown to black beans that are moist to the touch and pliable.

Watercress Slightly peppery salad leaf, rich in vitamin C and iron. As the name suggests, it is grown in wet conditions. Buy in crisp bunches, pick the leaves, and discard the tough stems.

Index

Guide to weights & measures

The conversions given in the recipes in this book are approximate. Whichever system you use, remember to follow it consistently, thereby ensuring that the proportions are consistent throughout a recipe.

Weights

Imperial	Metric
1/3 oz.	10 g
1/2 oz.	15 g
3/4 oz.	20 g
1 oz.	30 g
2 oz.	60 g
3 oz.	90 g
4 oz. (1/4 lb.)	125 g
5 oz. (1/3 lb.)	150 g
6 oz.	180 g
7 oz.	220 g
8 oz. (1/2 lb.)	250 g
9 oz.	280 g
10 oz.	300 g
11 oz.	330 g
12 oz. (3/4 lb.)	375 g
16 oz. (1 lb.)	500 g
2 lb.	1 kg
3 lb.	1.5 kg
4 lb.	2 kg

Volume

Imperial	Metric	Cup
1 fl. oz.	30 ml	
2 fl. oz.	60 ml	1/4
3 fl. oz.	90 ml	1/3
4 fl. oz.	125 ml	1/2
5 fl. oz.	150 ml	2/3
6 fl. oz.	180 ml	3/4
8 fl. oz.	250 ml	1
10 fl. oz.	300 ml	1 1/4
12 fl. oz.	375 ml	1 1/2
13 fl. oz.	400 ml	1 2/3
14 fl. oz.	440 ml	1 3/4
16 fl. oz.	500 ml	2
24 fl. oz.	750 ml	3
32 fl. oz.	1 L	4

Oven temperature guide

The Celsius (°C) and Fahrenheit (°F) temperatures in this chart apply to most electric ovens. Decrease by 25°F or 10°C for a gas oven or refer to the manufacturer's temperature guide. For temperatures below 325°F (160°C), do not decrease the given temperature.

Oven description	°C	°F	Gas Mark
Cool	110	225	1/4
	130	250	1/2
Very slow	140	275	1
	150	300	2
Slow	170	325	3
Moderate	180	350	4
	190	375	5
Moderately Hot	200	400	6
Fairly Hot	220	425	7
Hot	230	450	8
Very Hot	240	475	9
Extremely Hot	250	500	10

Useful conversions

1/4 teaspoon	1.25 ml
1/2 teaspoon	2.5 ml
1 teaspoon	5 ml
1 Australian tablespoon	20 ml (4 teaspoons)
1 UK/US tablespoon	15 ml (3 teaspoons)

Butter/Shortening

1 tablespoon	1/2 oz.	15 g
1 1/2 tablespoons	3/4 oz.	20 g
2 tablespoons	1 oz.	30 g
3 tablespoons	1 1/2 oz.	45 g